This World: A *Christian's Workshop*

This World:
A Christian's Workshop

With warm regards to one of my

BROOKS HAYS

favorite editors R. N. Owen

Brooks Hays

BROADMAN PRESS
Nashville, Tennessee

© 1958 Broadman Press
Nashville, Tennessee

422–07173

Library of Congress catalog card number: 58–13329
Printed in the United States of America
10.JE58K.S.P.

Contents

Dedicated to MY MOTHER AND FATHER, who gave me my first impressions of this world as a Christian's workshop

Foreword

This collection of speeches and articles covers a thirty-year period, beginning in 1929 about the time of my entry into Arkansas state politics. The selection of statements from the vast accumulation of words which a lawyer, particularly a Member of Congress, would inevitably use, was largely the work of Mrs. Helen Hill Miller and my legislative assistant, Warren I. Cikins. I trust that, considered together, these utterances faithfully reflect my conviction that our existence here on earth can be given significance through a struggle for the good life for all men. Viewed in this light, the world cannot be regarded as a secular interference with our individual Christian devotions but as the scene of moral exertions which God requires of us.

It will be noted that some of the words which follow Mrs. Miller's sketch, including the introductions to the chapters, are not my own. The brief contributions of others are designed to fortify my principal thesis. Some of the passages are intended to illustrate the difficulties which often confront "the political practitioner." There are painful dilemmas in public service which cannot be escaped. Former Congressman Jerry Voorhis used to say we should have the privilege of saying, "Mr. Speaker, I vote 51 per cent Aye and 49 per cent No." But we don't have that privilege, and I have done and said things that clearly demonstrate that the choice is often between alternatives, neither of which is ideal.

Perhaps the material chosen from the first period will appear to be technical and of limited interest. I hope that the reader will feel compensated by the subsequent chapters which were thought to have a certain timeliness.

I am grateful to Mrs. Miller and Mr. Cikins for their contribution to this book and to the members of my office staff, John S. McLees, Mrs. Lurlene Wilbert, Kitty Johnson, and Mrs. Lilyan Bailey, for their help in assembling and editing the articles and addresses.

BROOKS HAYS

Profile of a Man

HELEN HILL MILLER

The *Washington Evening Star* for June 13, 1922, carried a Berryman cartoon showing a competent-looking middle-aged man, in shirt sleeves, at his desk. Tapping him on the shoulder stood a bespectacled youth, diploma in hand. The youth was saying, "Now, Dad, you need a rest. I'm ready to take hold." Young Brooks Hays cut out the cartoon and pasted it in his scrapbook.

The week before, he had received his law diploma from George Washington University. His formal education was complete. For the past three years, he had financed night classes by working daytime, at the United States Treasury Department, in a job secured for him by Arkansas Congressman H. M. Jacoway. Today, he quips about the three years' employment: "All week long, eight hours a day, six days a week, I counted twenty-dollar bills and on Saturday night I got one of them."

Now he was a lawyer, all set to go back to Arkansas and practice. In February, he had married Marion Prather of Fort Smith; during their freshman year at the University of Arkansas they had met at a spelling bee of the Periclean Literary Society. He had ignored the fact that she was a Methodist while he was a Baptist. Now they were man and wife.

In the Russellville Baptist Church, where as a boy of eleven he had been baptized, he was ordained as a deacon in

1

1923, thereby validating the nickname by which he was known in college. The grandson of a Baptist preacher, he taught a Sunday school class while at the University of Arkansas, was president of the YMCA, and worked in a mission. Among the first to benefit from his talents as a speaker were local Baptist Young People's Union groups and county singing conventions.

On behalf of the newly formed partnership of Hays, Priddy, and Hays, announcement cards wished potential clients a Happy New Year in 1923, but the first thing that Brooks Hays did on his return to Russellville was to plunge into a political campaign. Steele Hays, his father, had decided to run for Congress; Brooks stumped for him. Steele Hays lost, but shortly before the primary he received from a venerable colleague, Colonel Marcellus Davis of Dardanelle, a heartwarming account of the effectiveness of his son: "I heard your boy speak yesterday afternoon. Under the conditions, of course, he didn't have a *big* crowd, but it was a listening outfit, and I don't think a man came away who didn't fairly tingle with pleasure, feeling completely rewarded. It was, I consider, a very, very delicate and difficult task, a boy speaking for his P-a-a. . . ."

Colonel Davis likewise gave the boy a hand when he lost his first case. A dog had been killed; on behalf of its plaintiff owner, Brooks planned a tear-jerking appeal, including recitation of the "Eulogy on the Dog" with which Missouri's Senator George Graham Vest had swayed another courtroom. But without letting Brooks get even to the first line, the judge dismissed the case on a technicality. From a front seat in the courtroom, Colonel Davis audibly remarked, "In my opinion, sir, you have committed grave error."

The case marked the beginning of two and a half years' practice in Russellville, during which Brooks was a joiner of joiners, taking part in every sort of community activity. He was elected secretary of the state Democratic convention, youngest man ever to hold the post. With the Eighteenth Amendment in force, he spoke at WCTU meetings. Initiated into the Masonic order, he began a progress which culminated in 1957 in election to the 33rd degree of Scottish Rite Masonry. His presidency of the local Lions Club led on to a district governorship in the International in 1926. Made eligible by army service in the autumn of 1918, he joined the American Legion; in 1945 he was asked by Legion officials to be a cosponsor in the House of Representatives of the legislation that became known as the GI Bill of Rights.

But there was one organization which in the mid-twenties had a wide following in the Russellville community that Brooks Hays did not join: the Klan. His diary for July 31, 1923 contains the entry:

Spent day in office. Ellsworth Coombs, head of state Ku Klux Klan, visited me in afternoon. He was disappointed when I told him I had been invited to introduce him at the meeting that night but had declined. I worked in three meetings, went to a short American Legion session first, then to the study course at the church, and was even able to hear Brother Coombs speak for half an hour at the Klan meeting. He failed to convince me that my first impression of the Klan was incorrect. The high place in his speech had an appeal to prejudice and vengeance. He left me unshaken in the view that individual members of the Klan would do better to put their energy into the church.

Betty Brooks Hays was born that October. When the little family was on vacation the next summer, a telephone call from his law partner, Judge Priddy, brought Brooks back into politics again. H. W. Applegate, candidate for attorney general, wanted him as campaign manager.

Applegate was elected, and promptly named Brooks as an

assistant attorney general. Two months before the birth of
Marion Steele Hays added a son to the family, the Hayses
moved from Russellville to Little Rock, and Brooks went
from private practice into public office, specializing in tax,
motor truck, and minimum wage legislation. When the constitutionality of Arkansas's $1.25-a-day wage for women was
challenged, Hays prepared the state's brief upholding it.
Though the situation was markedly parallel to the Washington state case that subsequently reversed the prevailing doctrine, the Federal district judge refused to upset the previous
Supreme Court ruling in the Children's Hospital case.

During this period, Hays drafted the legislation that gave
Arkansas its first public library law—to the pleasure of his
mother, who was particularly interested in libraries. He
spoke widely on prison reform. The *Pine Bluff Gazette* reported the twenty-seven-year-old attorney as affirming that
"the average age of the inmates of our penitentiary is twenty-
eight years. It is a proven fact that it is possible a man may
be plastic until thirty years old."

Then in 1928, after a brief period in the life insurance
business, Brooks Hays made his first incursion into politics
on his own behalf. At the age of twenty-nine, he ran for
governor.

The incumbent, Harvey Parnell, who as lieutenant governor had succeeded to the governorship when Governor Martineau became a Federal judge, was backed by an organization
based on an enormous highway construction program; the
contributions of the bond-brokers and the contractors were
far in excess of the $5,000 which was all that the Hayses, fa-
ther and son, could put together. Brooks Hays advocated
changes in the highway financing program, adoption of a
state income tax, construction of a new state hospital, state
aid for rural schools, and a program to bring industry to rural

areas. He carried the state capital and ran second in a field of seven; Parnell received less than a majority of the votes, but in the absence of a run-off primary—not adopted until 1933—became governor and at the next session of the state legislature put through a good part of Hays's platform proposals, including the state income tax, as his own.

In 1930, the governorship came up again; Hays, as the previous runner-up, was a logical opposition candidate. Advisers, including his father, thought him unlikely to win, and his Little Rock law firm, Hays and Turner, was certain to lose business if he announced. On the other hand, if he intended to stay in politics, he could hardly sidestep a challenge to an administration whose practices were unchanged from the previous contest. He made the race, polled 30,000 more votes than in 1928, once more carried the state capital, but came out second in a field of five.

Two years later, Brooks's former Russellville law partner, A. B. Priddy, decided to run, and though Brooks had given thought to a third try now that Parnell was through— he might even have had support from the outgoing governor —seniority prevailed, and Brooks backed Judge Priddy in his unsuccessful bid. However, in the same primary, he himself ran for Democratic national committeeman, carried 73 of the 75 counties, and served in his new capacity until 1939.

In the committee post, Brooks helped find funds for the 1932 Roosevelt campaign, and went avidly with a group of other state leaders to meet the Democratic candidate in St. Louis and turn over to him a check for $4,500, mostly raised by one-dollar sales of campaign buttons.

After the election, Brooks went to Washington to look for a Federal job in the executive branch. Cabinet member Frances Perkins offered to make him Assistant to the Secretary of Labor—he was president of the Arkansas Conference of Social Work at the time—but just then word came of the appointment to a Federal judgeship of the congressman from Arkansas's Fifth District. Since this district includes the Little Rock area where Brooks had always done very well, he decided to return home and run.

It was a disillusioning experience. The political leaders in one county had determined to count him out. When the votes were tallied, over the rest of the district Brooks led by 595 votes. Registration in the county where leaders opposed Brooks totalled 1,632. In spite of this maximum figure of legitimate ballots, the results were declared to be 1,850 votes for Hays's opponent, and 616 for Hays. And in spite of the self-evident character of the fraud, in the tedious lawsuit which followed, a series of technicalities prevented Brooks from obtaining a recount. As he walked alone to his office the evening the case was dismissed, a newsboy stopped him: "All about the election contest. Hays loses lawsuit. Want to know about it, don't you, mister?" Holding out a nickel, Hays said, "You'll never know how much I do know about it."

That nickel represented quite an investment. The year 1933 was a year of lean times for the country, and for the Hayses. Though the congressional fight had been financed mostly through small sums contributed by his friends, Brooks owed some $8,000 in obligations incurred during his previous campaigns. Law business was scarce. To get grocery money, Brooks taught evening classes in public speaking; one night a week he drove to Hot Springs for this purpose, in spite of the fact that after paying $1.00 for his hotel room and apologetically giving a nickel tip to the bellboy—who said he got a lot of nickel tips these days—he didn't do much more than break even. So in 1934 Brooks went back to Washington.

There, Arthur Altmeyer told him the post of labor compliance officer and legal adviser to the NRA director for Arkansas was open; it carried a salary of $4,500 a year. That meant that Brooks could not only support his family but pay off his obligations.

The job of getting acceptance in Arkansas for the minimum NRA code wage of 40¢ an hour was a tough one. Unemployment was so great that thousands of people were ready to work for anything they could get, and the employed in marginal industry were always subject to the competition of the *under*employed in marginal agriculture, eager to move to town and replace them.

Brooks's technique was to negotiate voluntary compliance wherever possible. The larger plants presented no very great difficulty. The harder case of the little man operating on the ragged edge of nothing was put by a sawmill operator from the western hill country, who came to Little Rock and confronted NRA's staff of three with the bitter comment: "You're tellin' me what *I've* got to do. Now you, and you, and you get a salary. Each of you has a check comin' the first of the month. You pay your grocery bills with it. But I got no salary. I don't get no regular check. What I've got to do is to keep a little mill runnin', an' there's thirteen families who get their groceries from workin' in it. *That's* what I've got to do!"

Arkansas's Senator Joe Robinson, who as Senate majority leader piloted the New Deal through Congress during "the hundred days," said once to Brooks Hays in a private conversation that he was proud of all the recovery programs except the NRA. Yet even granting the shakiness of both its constitutional and its economic basis, Brooks felt it accomplished some good during the grim months until at last an Arkansas courthouse hanger-on announced that the depression must be over—he'd seen a rabbit cross the road that morning without anybody after him.

In April, 1934, Brooks had a telegram from a person he'd never heard of but with whom he has since engaged in various joint projects over the years—Francis Pickens Miller of Virginia. Miller was inviting a cross-section group of Southerners concerned with regional issues to a session in Atlanta. There, they initiated the Southern Policy Committee, which from 1936 until the outbreak of World War II held annual meetings to consider problems (1) of Southern agriculture—the Bankhead-Jones Act, farm tenancy; (2) of Southern industry—wage and hour legislation, social security, the TVA; and (3) the need for wider political participation. (The Southern Policy Committee has sometimes been confused with the Southern Conference on Human Welfare, the ill-fated organization which grew out of a Birmingham meeting in 1939 and was taken over by fellow travelers when its excesses made it impossible for Southern moderates to influence policies.)

In 1935, Will W. Alexander, a Missouri native who knew marginal agriculture in his Ozark boyhood and who had for years headed the Interracial Commission in Atlanta, asked Brooks to join him in Washington; he was then Assistant Administrator of the Resettlement Administration and later became Administrator of the Farm Security Administration. For two years, Brooks spent most of his time in Washington, though after the election of his friend Carl Bailey to the Arkansas governorship in 1936 he frequently acted as the governor's adviser in federal-state relationships. Under Governor Bailey, Arkansas was the first state to adopt a model soil conservation law.

After Senator Robinson's death in July, 1937, however, Governor Bailey attempted to go to the Senate but made the mistake of asking for the nomination from the state Democratic committee rather than offering himself to the electorate in a primary. Popular disapproval of this procedure caused his defeat by John E. Miller in November and carried Brooks, along with others of his supporters, into political eclipse. Brooks transferred to the Farm Security Administration's regional office in Little Rock as its attorney. For several years he was out of state politics, and in 1939 passage of the Hatch Act, forbidding political activity by Federal Government employees, made necessary his resignation from the Democratic National Committee also.

During this interval, he had an opportunity to see at the grass roots the difference that the new agricultural programs were making in the South's rural life. A teacher in a small rural school in Pulaski County summed it up when she asked her fifteen pupils: "Who is the President of the United States?" No answer. Finally one little boy raised his hand. "Jimmy, you tell us the President's name." "Miss Myrtle," he said, "I don't know who the President is, but Mr. Hannah is our Farm Security Administration supervisor."

At the same time, Brooks resumed his civic activities and gave increasing time to his church. During the latter 1920's and early '30's he had headed Little Rock's 1929 Community Chest drive, cutting administrative costs by a third while raising a maximum budget; he had directed a series of surveys for the statewide Baptist Rural Church Commission, whose organization he had proposed in 1929, and prepared a report for the Pulaski County Hospital Committee with regard to institutional care of the aged and indigent; he had helped Little Rock's Negro leaders form an Urban League in the interest of social welfare activities for Negroes; he had taught the Bible class in Little Rock's Second Baptist Church which today still bears his name.

In April, 1942, he decided to return to politics and again contested the Congressional seat for which he had been a candidate nearly a decade earlier. This time he won, and through eight consecutive terms he has since continued as the representative of the Fifth District's six counties in the center of the state including the state capital.

The 1942 victory was a welcome change in the Hays fortunes. The desperate last-minute effort of his opposition to exploit race feeling by charging that Hays would seek dangerous alterations in the South's social patterns had little effect upon the election results. Even the county which had produced his 1933 election tragedy turned in a majority for him.

Congress does its work through committees; assignments for Hays began with a seat on the House Banking and Currency Committee; there, between the end of the war and 1951, he participated in threshing out big domestic issues— price controls, commodity concessions, living costs—and felt the full impact of lobbies based in his state—cotton, oil, natural gas, utilities, which sometimes sought what Hays regarded as unjustifiable exceptions in price control policies.

In 1951 he transferred from the Banking and Currency Committee to the Foreign Affairs Committee, where he is now the fifth ranking member. Among special committee assignments, he served on the Select Committee to Investigate Tax-exempt Foundations in the 82nd Congress, and the Commission on Intergovernmental Relations headed by Meyer Kestnbaum during the 83rd and 84th Congresses. In 1958 Speaker Rayburn appointed Brooks to the "blue ribbon" committee to study problems of "space exploration and astronautics."

Over his years in Congress, three main subjects have claimed a large part of Hays's time and interest: rural life, foreign affairs, and civil rights.

In promoting legislation to strengthen family-size farm life and aid low income farm people, Hays carried into governmental life his strong concern for a neglected group with which so much of his early life had been identified. This interest found expression in his sponsorship of a bill which became law to require the sale of surplus government farm land in family tracts to farm veterans (his first legislative triumph). With Senator Flanders of Vermont as cosponsor, he has urged policies in behalf of small rural industries and establishment of a presidential commission on rural life.

Closely related to this activity has been his espousal of a program for the development of the Arkansas River Valley resources.

In the foreign affairs field, he has been a proponent of bipartisanship, of the United Nations, of broad measures of foreign co-operation and foreign aid.

His attitude on civil rights has developed through long experience. During the 1930's, he was a proponent of repeal of poll tax laws, in the states that still had them, as a prerequisite to voting. At the same time, he had direct experience of interracial conciliation in both his NRA and FSA work, witnessing the mutually beneficial improvement of the economic situation in his area among both white and colored citizens. (The young colored man to whom, during the depression, the Hayses rented for 50¢ a week the room in which they no longer kept a maid, now operates one of Little Rock's substantial trucking businesses.) He has always believed in an approach to change based on local consent, but he has likewise believed that a broadened basis of consent needs constantly to be sought for changes that are inevitable concomitants of economic development.

As a result, in 1949 when the Truman civil rights bill was introduced as a follow-up of the Democratic platform commitments of 1948, Hays countered with a proposal which sought:

> Elimination, through constitutional amendment, of the poll tax as a prerequisite to voting;
>
> Desegregation of interstate travel by Federal statute;
>
> Provision for Federal action in cases of lynching when, as, and if local authorities failed to exercise their responsibilities;
>
> Establishment of a service in the Department of Labor which would seek to negotiate voluntary adoption of fair employment practices, in a manner comparable to existing efforts to encourage more general hiring of the physically handicapped.

Neither this alternative nor that proposed by the Administration became law, but the Hays proposal attracted wide attention as a possible middle ground between opposing political factions.

Largely because of this background, when the civil rights plank became a central issue prior to the 1952 Democratic convention, Hays was made a member of the preconvention platform committee, and was one of the key negotiators who, with Senator Humphrey as spokesman for the Northern liberal attitude and Senator Sparkman as the representative of the moderate Southern view, worked out a wording of the platform plank which made possible a united party. In 1956, Hays was a member of the platform committee, this time as an Arkansas delegate.

Because of his concern for local due process, Hays voted against the civil rights act of 1957 in its final form. He announced that had the jury trial provision for all cases, as contained in the Senate version, been maintained by the House-Senate conference that shaped the final bill, he would have assented to it, but he felt that the judicial discretion allowed in minor cases under the final act transgressed this principle.

Then at the end of the 1957 summer the painful events at Little Rock brought Hays into a new kind of national prominence.

When Sherman Adams, now Assistant to the President, served as a Republican member of Congress from New Hampshire in the 1940's, his office was close to Hays's in the Old House Office Building, and though from different parties, the two became good friends and saw each other frequently. Therefore, when the Little Rock crisis of September forced choices upon President Eisenhower, Hays found no difficulty in initiating through Adams the meeting of the President and Governor Faubus at Newport, Rhode Island.

In foreign affairs, an area in which Hays has been particularly active, his record also goes back to the early years of his congressional service. In 1944, as a member of a congressional delegation visiting the European theater, through buzz-bombed nights he gained a first-hand impression of the economic devastation in England, saw the D-Day beaches in Normandy within short weeks after the landings there, and was in Paris shortly after liberation. Another member of this group was Republican Congressman Walter Judd of Minnesota, who, before coming to Congress, had been a medical missionary in China. Together, on their return, the two sponsored a resolution underlining the importance of bipartisanship in foreign affairs, and toured the country speaking on behalf of such an attitude.

Hays's voting record—from his wartime approval of UNRRA through postwar votes for the British loan, the Marshall Plan, Greek-Turkish aid, successive extension of the Reciprocal Trade Agreements Act, and successive continuances of foreign economic and military assistance and technical development of underdeveloped areas—has reflected a consistent purpose. In 1956 his handling of an important phase of the foreign aid bill staved off a crippling reduction, and in 1957 he won a rare word of commendation from House Speaker Sam Rayburn and a telephone call of thanks from the White House for his handling of the bill to extend the British loan.

This record has been the subject of some horseplay by his colleagues. When Brooks made his first appearance at the House Foreign Affairs Committee in 1951, the chairman, former Congressman J. P. Richards of South Carolina, introduced the new member by telling the witness before the Committee that morning, General George Marshall, "General, our new member, Mr. Hays, rode to the Capitol this morning on a cloud." But Brooks took it in stride: "You see, General Marshall, I believe that Congress, like your army, needs reconnaissance."

Foreign aid, coupled with the race question, has also been injected into various Arkansas political campaigns when Hays has sought re-election. In 1952, when he was opposed by Amis Guthridge, who is today an indefatigable speaker for White Citizens Councils, Guthridge told many audiences, "Mr. Hays's heart bleeds for Afghanistan." After his 37,000 to 21,000 victory over Guthridge, Hays told the Afghanistan Minister in Washington that the people of his district clearly did not think it disqualified a man for congressional service to have an interest in his people.

In 1955, as a member of the United States delegation to the UN, Hays had direct experience with the difficulties of making progress in world affairs, and particularly in dealing with Russian delegates. At that time, the Russians were pressing for admission to the UN of various of their satellites, including Outer Mongolia, as independent countries. Hays told one of his Russian colleagues that he was entirely agreeable to the admission of Outer Mongolia if, in return, the

Russians would accept Texas as an independent member. Texas, he said, was quite as independent of the United States as Outer Mongolia was of the USSR, and at the same time was quite as likely to be loyal. Of course, Hays added, while they were about it they might as well change the name of Texas to Outer Arkansas.

Paralleling his congressional activities, Brooks Hays has consistently maintained his church interests. On his wartime trip to Europe, he met in London with Dr. J. H. Rushbrooke, president of the Baptist World Alliance, and became the intermediary for the re-establishment of contact with the French Baptists, of whom the Alliance office had had no word since the Nazis occupied Paris.

On this same trip, after a briefing by General Eisenhower at SHAEF headquarters, the group of Congressmen were housed in Cherbourg in what had until very recently been the German staff headquarters. There Hays found two books, one a German Bible and the other a book of personal devotions inscribed to their pastor by the Ladies' Aid of a Düsseldorf church. Through a German churchman who visited the United States several years later, he traced the owner, Dr. Alvin Ahlbory, a wartime chaplain in the German army. When he wrote Ahlbory preparatory to returning the books, the pastor asked him to keep the Bible as a symbol of Christian faith transcending political boundaries. In 1951, when Hays was a member of a House Foreign Affairs subcommittee visiting Germany to consult with Ernst Reuter of Berlin and Chancellor Adenauer, at a dinner given for the visitors in Frankfurt, Hays and Ahlbory met, and the incident transcended the evening's political news in the headlines.

In 1949, following a suggestion of Senator Mike Monroney, Hays introduced in the House a resolution to provide a meditation and prayer room at the Capitol. The resolution was ultimately approved unanimously by both Houses, and in March, 1955, the prayer room, for use exclusively by members of Congress, became a reality.

Over the postwar period, Hays has been a frequent speaker at meetings of the National Conference of Christians and Jews, organized by a group that included a fellow Baptist, Charles E. Hughes, and a fellow Democrat, Newton D. Baker, to strengthen and protect civic and political rights by the united efforts of religiously motivated citizens. Hays, having remained a loyal Democrat in the Smith-Hoover presidential contest, was very conscious of its value. At the same time, he took vigorous issue with those who complained about ministers "getting out of their place" in opposing Al Smith. "Let them stick to the gospel" was the theme of some Democratic speakers. Hays declared: "It is better for a minister to be wrong on specific issues than to say he has no message for the world." It was the beginning of his long insistence that no social, economic, or political pressures should ever be applied to prevent a minister from saying what his conscience directs.

In later years he was equally clear as to the importance of the world brotherhood movement. When at NATO headquarters in 1951, he discussed with General Eisenhower the necessity for moral and spiritual parallels to physical and military might. Speaking at a national conference at Pittsburgh in 1954, he stressed the necessity for a social fabric to underlying law:

Government and religion are interrelated, though the symbols and phrases are different. Government says "justice"; religion says "mercy." Government says "union," for we must think in structural terms; religion says "unity," for spiritual force must supply the quality that gives strength and cohesiveness to our legal institutions. Government says "power"; religion says "responsibility";

for power must be used with a sense of dedication. Government says "order," for none of the incidents of an enriching and satisfying society can be maintained except as we are free from violence. But religion says "discipline," and only the inner disciplines that spring from a life of faith can sustain external order. Finally, government says "tolerance" but religion says "love."

In his own denomination, Hays was elected to its second vice-presidency in 1951, and became first a member and then chairman of the Convention's Christian Life Commission, on whose behalf he transmitted to the 1957 assembly the report on race relations, which has been widely distributed throughout the South. Speaking of this commission's work at the Kansas City meeting of the Convention in 1956, Hays said:

The Christian Life Commission is coming of age. There have been stages in its growth when it was viewed rather skeptically. The timidity which has at times accompanied the response to our summons to service seems to be vanishing; we are being accepted. There is an element of promotion in our present endeavors. The grand idea which we seek to sustain, that of projecting the law of love and the ideal of Christian service into the life of our world, though not always consistently embraced by our people, is thoroughly in accord with our tradition and history. The meditations by our leadership and the rank and file produced a definite decision upon this fateful question of whether or not the waiting and suffering world is to have a clear voice and a bold purpose on the part of this mighty organization. In our great dilemmas of the past the right decisions have been made, sometimes at a painful cost, for differences in conviction have produced in the congregational forms of church government the divisiveness that is a part of the price we pay for democracy. . . . Ours is a broad fellowship embracing a great diversity of political and social viewpoints, and this quality in our denomination life is to be kept in mind in our operations. Nevertheless, in stimulating the ideals of human service, we seek to avoid diluting convictions. We would be unworthy of your confidence were we to let considerations of expediency determine our policies. Moral mediocrity should never characterize a Baptist agency.

Then in May, 1957, when the Southern Baptist Convention chose its president for the coming year, for the sixth time in its 113-year history, a layman was elected to preside over the more than eight million members—Brooks Hays of Arkansas. In this responsible post, Hays made it his purpose to consult with a maximum number of congregations and state associations, and through the ensuing year he visited churches and state and regional conferences in every part of the Convention's territory.

Together with Dr. Clarence W. Cranford, president of the American Baptist Convention, in April of 1958 he made a journey to Russia to bring fraternal greetings to the more than one-half million Baptists in the USSR, returning the visit of five of their members to the United States in 1956.

In his presidential address at Houston in May, 1958, where he was re-elected for a second term as president, Hays said these words from which the title of this book is taken:

In my boyhood I avoided confusion about God's attitude toward this world by assuming that when a minister said that I should "despise the world" he meant I should despise "worldliness." The Bible told me that God "loved the world." I thrilled to the song "This Is My Father's World" and to the words of our beloved Dr. George W. Truett, "It was deliberately in the mind of God not to reveal very much to us of the other world because he did not propose to detract from the critical importance of *this* earthly existence." If our Christian doctrines regarding God, the world, and man are to be taken seriously, it is apparent that this world is a Christian's workshop.

I

Southern People: Their Land and Their Income

From the time that Brooks Hays hung out his lawyer's shingle and went into state politics, means of offering greater opportunity to Arkansas people and people of the Southern regions generally have been of continual concern to him. Diversification of agriculture, introduction of industry, conservation of the soil, and improvement of systems of land tenure have claimed his specific attention.

❖

Why Industry?

Industry" is the chief topic in almost every gathering of businessmen or civic leaders—the most absorbing theme of Arkansas economists and public men. But in spite of the enthusiasm for industry among our businessmen, especially those who have studied the question closely, there are a number of men of influence, who, if not openly hostile to an industrial life of Arkansas, are inquiringly concerned over a movement which will affect our social structure so materially. Not long ago, I heard a lawyer say, "No! No! Not industry—it means smoke and dirt and bad living conditions. Let's stay agricultural; let's be individualists; the industrial barons will ruin us." A large plantation owner also openly opposed industrial expansion. Thus, I doubt if our people are thoroughly converted to the efficacy of the industrial program.

NOTE: This was published in the *Arkansas Banker* for March, 1929.

For example, the commercial organizations of a few Arkansas towns have apparently turned their backs upon industrial progress, continuing to stress as of first importance a purely agricultural program. This is defended upon the ground that the towns are, in fact, unselfishly interested in the welfare of rural populations and recognize a duty in this respect. We may well ask, it seems to me, if those leaders who are responsible for shifting emphasis from proposed industrial expansion see the farmers' problems in the larger aspect, that is, in relation to our whole economic life—market as well as yield—purchasing power as well as efficiency in crop production. The farmer has been swept into a complex economic life and he must either control to a degree, or compromise with, forces which have obviously been hostile to him.

There need be no quarrel between industry and agriculture. The simple point is this—the businessman, it seems, can be of greater service to the farmer, can get greater returns from the effort, by supporting a sound industrial program for his community. To be sure, I believe it is the businessman's duty to support the splendid forward-looking agricultural program of our various agencies, and with so much educational work to be done, it is gratifying to see the bankers of Arkansas assuming a part in this. Many products of our modern life give to the town man and the farmer a common viewpoint. The agricultural extension forces of the University, for example, must find the keen interest of Arkansas's businessmen in rural problems a great stimulus. But we are interested in the matter of emphasis—where shall emphasis be placed—upon agricultural programs, or upon industry, and why?

Arkansas, classified as rural, not urban, may boast of its towns. The state is filled with towns, and that part of our present social system we want to see preserved. The good roads are strengthening the larger towns, and this in time means fewer towns, but not necessarily a continuing urbanization. And what of the future of the small town? Their leaders were pleased with the recent assertion of Henry Ford, that "industry favors the town—will be the small town's salvation in the new industrial age." This is good news, and the town man must conclude from this that industry is entitled not merely to good will, a pat on the back, but positive support.

. . . Thousands of Arkansas men and women, we are told, walk the streets of Arkansas towns today, looking for employment. Many of these have come in from the country because there was nothing back there to attract them. Moreover, they wanted better schools and churches than their rural environment afforded. Men will make terrific sacrifices in order that their children may have good school and church advantages. The skeptic who fears industrial life because of social conditions will concede that the preservation and expansion of our sturdy religious life and the strengthening of our school system contemporaneously with industrial development will protect us against anything sinister in social developments.

Rev. J. W. Speake, pastor of the St. Paul Methodist Church in Greenville, South Carolina, observing conditions in his own city, stated in a recent article in the *Manufacturers' Record:*

The writer of this article lives in a town on the outskirts of which is a school district that enrolls more than 5,000 white children; more than any other district in the state; children of industry, all of them; "Anglo-Saxon," whatever that may mean. Nearly all are adherents of one or two Protestant churches. More children here than are found in any one of 31 counties in the state. The church of their choosing can have them any day in the year for religious training and instruction when the church is prepared to give adequate instruction. I submit that nowhere else on the top side of this world is there a like opportunity.

Also bearing testimony to the effect of industry upon the religious life of the people, Wade H. Harris observes that

No labor in the world is more responsive to the advantages of its surroundings. The mill help in the South attends the finest churches in the section; a church for each denomination. With the best preachers that can be drawn from Convention, Conference, Association or Synod. The children of the mill people have the advantages of standard schools, with longer terms and with better paid teachers than are provided in state schools or in schools maintained by municipalities. They have Young Men's and Young Women's Christian Associations, community houses, gymnasiums, ball grounds, play grounds, and recreation parks. Around every house is a plot of land from which garden truck is supplied the year around. The front yards are converted into flower gardens, and the annual flower show staged by the mill people is an event in all Southern textile communities.

. . . That prosperity resulting from industrial development does not produce indifference to spiritual life is reflected in the comparison of investments in church property in North Carolina with that in our own state. For example, Arkansas Baptists had invested in church property in 1910, $1,515,-355.00. In 1927, investments amounted to $5,307,511.00, representing an increase of $3,792,156.00. Note, however, the corresponding increase in the state of North Carolina, in this year of industrial progress. In 1910, North Carolina Baptists had invested in church property $3,305,325.00, while in 1927 this had grown to the staggering sum of $22,459,724.00. In other words, while we were gaining $3,792,156.00, our sister state, which had little advantage over us in population in 1910, gained $19,154,399.00. Although Arkansas Baptists invested heavily in institutions of higher learning, enjoying in this period an increase of $1,532,885.02, our North Carolina brethren were gaining $5,924,836.11 in the same type of church investment, having in 1927 in college property and endowment a total of $6,874,730.11 against our $1,832,-885.02, all of which leads us to believe that prosperity does not destroy appreciation of the intangible values in life. In short, North Carolina Baptists have contributed to the church because they were able to contribute, and no state can expect a rapid advancement in religious and educational investments unless the people generally are enjoying the sort of prosperity which makes possible the advancement which we wish for in Arkansas.

I learn that the Methodist Church has enjoyed the same growth, and the figures for these two denominations manifestly reflect an enlarged spiritual life in the industrial state of North Carolina. The value of Methodist Church property in Arkansas in 1918 was $2,690,824,00. Ten years later, this had increased to $7,302,388.00, but in the same period North Carolina Methodists had increased their investment from $6,-370,464.00 to $20,405,193.00. The Methodists of Arkansas may well be proud of their present college endowments, totaling $1,159,092.00; but their industrial brethren in North Carolina boast of Methodist college endowments of $21,236,-552.00.

That there is direct relation between the industrial movement and this remarkable increase in religious and educational investments can not be questioned. The people of North Carolina recognize in the social progress of the state the greatest benefits, perhaps, of the industrial era.

. . . In pointing to the advantages of industrial development, I do not, of course, suggest that the state can afford to destroy by legislation or otherwise the measures which are found to be necessary for protection against unwarranted business activity, nor should we by engaging in a frenzied effort to induce outside capital to come into the state, sacrifice the interests of our own people. This article deals only with the salutary results to be expected from a sane and conservative program of industrial expansion for the state.

It is my firm conviction that all differences can be harmonized. We must first of all be interested in the *why* of industrial expansion—this we shall agree, is that our people may have larger incomes. Then those of us who are concerned about schools and social conditions—and that must surely include all—will assume our responsibility for seeing that our wealth does not spoil us; that our industry shall be a humanized industry; and that our people shall not become worshipers of materialism—preserving rather our present estimate of what constitute the finest things of life.

❖

Farm Tenancy and the Christian Conscience

I am not going to talk to you today as an expert because I am not an expert, but I do want to talk to you out of my own experiences about a problem that the nation is becoming very much interested in, that is, the problem of farm tenancy. What shall we do about tenancy? No one has a short answer for that question, but there are certain considerations to be

NOTE: Address for the annual dinner of the Christian Rural Fellowship, New York City, December 5, 1935.

kept clearly in mind as we search for the solution. We have first of all to think about the physical values that are involved. It is estimated that between thirty-five and fifty million acres of once productive land have been destroyed by water and dust erosion, and that these acres will probably never be useful again, at least not in our generation. In addition to this there is an impairment of one hundred and twenty-five million acres that a few years ago were not affected by erosion.

. . . In the complexities of the modern scene we assert the need of an ethical basis for a new land policy. We believe there is a definite spiritual aspect to the farm problem, and we agree with the proposition in Henry Wallace's speech before the land grant college presidents a month or two ago that at the end of all these efforts in the economic and political realm is a great abstraction. It is not necessary for me to put it in words—in fact Henry Wallace found it very difficult to do that—but it seems to me that this is a good starting point when we are talking about farmers and their troubles, particularly about the tenant farmers.

. . . In recent months I have covered quite a bit of the Ozark country and I tell you today that the people of those mountains are not the happy and carefree folk that are often pictured to you. There are certain compensations, of course, for their lack of a cash income, but they are really in trouble. Their fields have eroded, the soil's fertility is vanishing, their markets have all but disappeared, and the institutions which they once enjoyed, their schools and churches, have suffered terrifically. It is a very sensible thing which the Resettlement Administration undertakes when it seeks to relocate some of these families on land which will produce a fair living in communities where schools and churches may be provided, the children reared under normal conditions.

. . . That the rural slums extend into sections that never knew their blight until a few years ago can hardly be questioned now. The other day I came across some figures on family income for a group to be serviced by the Resettlement Administration. We found scores of families who had had cash incomes of less than $75 last year. The wisdom of making a change must be apparent. Society has paid a big relief bill because we wanted no one to starve, and as I have pointed out, the crime bill which the local communities must bear is certainly an inflated one. Moreover, the lands from which they have sought to make a living can more profitably be devoted to forestry, grazing, and recreation. It seems to make a clear case for resettlement. This obviously does not mean wholesale evacuation. There are splendid little valleys to be utilized. There is potential employment in the sound forestry program that is now being worked out.

. . . Strangely enough, many farms are held by corporations and some of that land could be purchased for individual families if the credit facilities were available. The pending Bankhead-Jones Farm Homes Bill would establish such facilities by providing for government loans upon very liberal repayment terms. Thus the method by which Denmark and Ireland reduced farm tenancy might be adopted in America. The bill has passed the Senate and has strong support in the House of Representatives. Favorable action by the House is hoped for at this session. A land ownership program such as contemplated by this measure is an extension (but a necessary extension) of the Resettlement idea. The bill should receive strong support from every section of the country.

The farm tenancy evil extends to every state in the union and even in New England there was a pronounced increase in tenancy between 1930 and 1935. For the United States as a whole it may be said that about fifty out of every hundred farmers are tilling rented land. While the condition is most acute in the cotton country, the wheat and corn belts are experiencing a rapid increase in farm tenancy. Iowa has a greater degree of tenancy than Tennessee. Indiana has passed Florida, and Minnesota's tenancy ratio exceeds Virginia's. The excess is slight in each case, but it demonstrates that this is not any longer a sectional problem. The race aspect is still important but the white race is now more vitally affected than the Negro. While the number of Negro tenants did not increase between 1920 and 1930, there was a 60 per cent increase in the number of white croppers. Still there are 700,000 Negro tenants in the United States and we have a problem here to engage the best effort of our leadership, both white and colored.

Surely there can be no question about the wisdom of changing from the absentee ownership type of farm operation to the resident type. Absentee ownership means the continuation of poverty. It is the curse of Southern agriculture.

The Christian conscience is needed in this task of getting the right viewpoint about land tenure. Man's relationship to the soil is still a challenging problem. Lives have been worn out in the effort to secure "title," and often after a bitter struggle it proved to be valueless. Title sometimes becomes an abstract thing. We know that value of ownership depends upon many factors in addition to the quality of soil.

. . . The Christian mind rebels against absentee ownership. The Christian mind rebels against the holding of land by wealthy men for recreation purposes if it be land that is adaptable to family-size farm operation and needed for that purpose. We are going to talk about these practices until they are outlawed.

Along with the destruction of false ideas about land and its

control there should be confidence in the possibilities of co-
operative effort making available credit at a reasonable rate
of interest and providing commissary and other services at
fair prices. The establishment of adequate church and school
facilities will continue to engage Christian thought. All these
are component parts of a rounded out rural program.

. . . I insist that whenever changes are made they should
be made with a sense of the ethical considerations that are
involved in this troublesome question. Man is the center of
our interest. His welfare is above everything else. It is with
that idea that the demand comes for a new land policy that
will be based upon the desire to secure the most efficient cultivation of all available acres for the good of those who have
a claim to participation in the land's benefits with a sense of
obligation to those who are not directly related to the soil.

❖

The Problem of the South's
Low Income Farmer

The subject, "The Problem of the South's Low Income
Farmer," opens the door to an important section of Southern
life. At the very bottom of our system is an economically sub-
merged group whose claim upon us is not to rest exclusively
on humanitarianism. I refer to the tenants, the croppers,
the submarginal landowners, and the day laborers of the
South. It is hardly accurate to say that they are forgotten
men because in recent years there has been a good deal of talk
about their condition. Though not forgotten they still may

NOTE: Address before the Members' Council of the New Orleans Association of Commerce, April 27, 1939.

be said to present the most appealing problem of all the dis-
advantaged groups.

It is anomalous that the benefits of the extensive relief and
reform legislative measures of the last few years have not
been extended to a group which probably stands in greatest
need of these benefits. The explanation is in administrative
difficulties and not in a lack of interest on the part of those
who framed significant social legislation, but the fact remains that the classes of the farm groups I have described do
not participate in the Social Security Act, the Wage and Hour
Act, and only to a very slight extent in the benefits of the
various housing acts. Furthermore, while other groups
within the agricultural population have been able to improve
their condition as a result of membership in powerful farm
organizations, the labor groups have derived very little benefit from organization.

. . . The expression "low income farmer" embraces many
classes. The term "tenancy" is the common symbol but in a
technical sense it is not acceptable. There are sections of the
South in which the tenant owns considerable equipment and
his economic situation is relatively good. On the other hand,
there are multitudes of small farm owners, particularly in the
hill country, who are fighting desperately to retain their stake
and to advance their level of living to include decent shelter,
nourishment, and medical services.

. . . The South is divided into two distinct sections, the
hill country and the fertile lowlands. From the standpoint of
human resources the hill country has been the most important
and every state in the South except Florida has its high land.
Unlike the Hebrew children who moved from fertile Goshen
to the Judean hills, our migrations in recent years have been
from eroding upland to the crowded delta. The impact of
this movement has not yet been fully felt. The hillbilly has

made his contribution to the low country and he has also created a problem. Before erosion took its toll, his mountain villages were filled with efficient social institutions. His schools and churches, while never flush with revenue, still did their work well. Extensive areas peopled a generation ago by independent and stable citizens now embrace a disintegrating rural life and those who remain constitute a social problem which the South can no longer ignore. The upland society produced great businessmen, statesmen, preachers, and professional men, and the cities today are peopled with its products. The fact that many successful men come out of this group ought to be sufficient answer to those who insist that the problems with which we are dealing are due to a class shiftlessness and lack of ability. One cannot altogether dispose of social problems by dealing with environment; nevertheless, the achievements of individual members of these groups supply ample evidence that there is basic character in the group.

. . . Let me concede at the outset that the problem is too complicated to admit offering a simple solution. Our thinking on this problem of relationships, owner-renter-furnisher-laborer, within the agricultural structure is still confused and the value of discussions of this type is in acquainting ourselves with the present picture. We have, first, the problem of finding enough land for those who must live upon it and from it. One-half of all the farmers of America are in the South, but we have little more than one-fourth of the nation's area. In the cotton South, embracing ten states, the average number of acres per capita in crops is eight, but in the thirty-eight other states it is just double that number, sixteen. More than one-fourth of our farmers have holdings of less than twenty acres. On the income side, we see the same pronounced disparities. The gross farm income per capita in the cotton states

is $194.00, in the other states it is $315.00 (1939). Sixty-
one per cent of the eroded area in the United States is in the
South. Still, agriculture is our basic industry; 44 per cent of
all gainfully employed are directly engaged in that industry,
and 70 per cent of our people are living in towns and open
country. It does not take statistics and studies to prove that
the countryside is crowded; we are a land-hungry people!

The population problem has a bearing. The rural South
has 17 per cent of the nation's children but has only 2 per
cent of the nation's income with which to educate them.
Congressman Patrick said, "The stork and the wolf always
did pal around together. While the old man is beating the
wolf off at the back door, the stork is fluttering down the
chimney in the front room."

. . . Displaced tenants from the South are going in large
numbers to California. The West Coast labor problem comes
into the discussion not because we are directly concerned
with the acute relief problem which that region confronts but
because of what it signifies as to the changes in Southern
economy. The rapid mechanization of cotton growing in the
Southwest, coupled with the effects of droughts which followed machine type commercial farming, has driven so
many farmers to the "land of sunshine and prosperity" that
the Californians have a new word for the transient agricultural worker. They assume he is from Oklahoma and these
workers are called "Okies." (If they find he is from my state,
and the Arkansawyers are pretty numerous out there, they
find it easy to switch over to "Arkies.")

One difficulty is the fact that tenants are constantly on the
move. More than 900,000 tenants in America moved last
year and the majority of those families were in the South.
There is an old saying that three moves equal one fire, and
with the average occupancy only three years it can be seen

there is a terrific loss from this practice. Displacement of tenants has clearly accentuated this practice, and even though the use of machinery does not altogether displace the family, it may mean a change of status and consequently a lower income. If a tenant earns from $500 to $1,000 annually, he may as an agricultural laborer not expect to earn more than from $200 to $300. A daily wage of 60¢ is not uncommon and the day's work seldom brings more than $1.00. Thus the farm worker's family cannot possibly expect to secure from farm employment in the working season enough to maintain a decent standard of living.

. . . Economic forces, of course, have a way of breaking down resistance, and if it were determined in any agricultural group that cotton picking machines were not to be tolerated because of the effect on unemployment, cotton picking machines would still be invented and manufactured and used when the economics of the situation justified it. It would certainly not be fair to the cotton growers of the South to say they should fight against anything that reduces costs, for their price situation is such that they must struggle for a wider margin of profit. For the industry as a whole, of course, the word "profit" is used in a liberal sense because, except for a few short intervals, the business has been profitless for a long time. I think this needs to be taken into consideration in all discussions of the human aspects of the region's problem. The cotton farmer, tenant or owner, white or Negro, needs more income, but the ceiling looks pretty low for the next few years, and we are forced to think not in terms of rapid boosting of cash income or not alone of a transition from tenant farming to owner-operator types but rather of improving human relationships and making our program for the region's advancement flexible enough to make an immediate improvement in living standards by gardening and diversification, also by supplementing farm income with other employment where possible.

Let us look at the things that are already being done by the Government under the sponsorship of the Farm Security Administration. In the middle of the depression, America was startled to find that almost a million farm families were on relief. We were accustomed to thinking that only in the cities could real deprivation exist. We thought that food could be found in abundance back on the farms and that the other primary needs, shelter, clothing, and medical care, would make such light demands in the way of cash outlay that no farm family could be in real want. This was not true, of course. The first decision regarding the problem was a fine one. It led to the program known as "rehabilitation" and involved a farm and home management plan for each family with the thought that all money put into the family's rehabilitation would be repaid. In other words, it was a loan and not a relief program. The loans for operating expenses are for one year and for equipment and capital goods of all kinds for five years. The Farm Security Administration has loaned in this way a total of 250 million dollars and although most of these loans will not be due for three or four years about 75 million dollars have already been repaid.

The Administration found not only that there are hundreds of thousands of farm families suffering from lack of credit but that poor health constituted a major handicap which could not be overcome except by careful planning and aid in the way of loans for medical services. This medical aid program is a very important one. Health factors can be measured in economic terms and those agencies which deal officially with health have commended the program which I am now describing. We have a high percentage of pellagra, malaria, tuberculosis, syphilis, and even hookworm in some communities, as well as many minor ailments to contend with. The cost of malaria in the whole South is said to be 500 million dollars a year and the economic loss of these other diseases is very great. Enough surveys have already been made as to the result of our rehabilitation work to prove that the health of the families is vitally affected. In a study of 20,000 families in the cotton South, it was shown that the average net worth of the families' goods when the program began in 1935 was only $2.00 and that it increased to more than $350.00 in 1937. In this two-year period attention was given to the health of the children, and it was interesting to find that the average daily school attendance of the children of these families exceeded that of the other children in the community. Loans for medical treatment are sometimes made on the basis of joint arrangements of individual families with members of parish and state medical societies whereby all the families in the group can be assured of medical services by a physician of their choice.

Other important phases of the Farm Security Administration program are tenant purchase loans authorized by the Bankhead-Jones Farm Tenant Act, and it is hoped over a period of time to greatly reduce farm tenancy throughout the South. The region has a big stake in this effort. During the current year we will lend money to approximately 1,100 families for the purchase of farms.

. . . This great metropolis already feels the effects of the economic forces treated in this talk. Let me repeat that purchasing power is the key to the solution, and if the city is to become the city of your dreams either in material power or from the standpoint of culture and social leadership, the needs of the outlying rural districts must be met. The entire South is proud of this city's history and commercial achievements and we have a tremendous interest in its future. You cannot build a great city and we cannot build a great South on peasantry. The trend toward that condition has been arrested, and with sustained support from business and political leaders this forward-looking rural program can be made a glorious success.

❖

The Christian's Relation to Land

There is an old adage that the lawyers like to quote: "Social opinion should always be in advance of law, and the greater or less happiness of the people depends upon the narrowness of the gulf between them." The Christian's interest in land is, therefore, centered less in legal concepts than the moral principles which underlie them. The Christian's hope for ethical relationship requires that the law retain its flexible and dynamic character, that legal formulations be responsive to human needs, and that educational groundwork for legal reforms be ethically directed.

It is the purpose of this article to deal broadly with the relations involved in land tenure and crop cultivation. Considering first the primary idea of ultimate ownership, to whom does land belong? According to the psalmist, "the earth is the Lord's," and in the sense that all resources which man controls should be impressed with a sense of stewardship, this is the first rule for the Christian. Its legal parallel is the common-law view that all land is subject to social control. To paraphrase the Hebrew statement, "The earth belongs to God's children." This is not too loose an application of the

NOTE: Address at the seventh annual meeting of the Christian Rural Fellowship, Nashville, Tennessee, October 22, 1941.

Scripture, for all through the Bible it is apparent that a fruitful and humanitarian use is expected of those who possess the Lord's earth.

It is utterly impossible to conceive of ownership except in relation to man. Individual claim to particular parts of these resources is recognized because of the ethical claim which springs out of certain services and for the further reason that limited individual ownership is an effective device for the proper use of the land.

The Christian religion is one of justice and right dealing, and these elements must characterize the Christian's attitude. While society's claims must be recognized, the rights of individuals must also be recognized, and it is Christianity's duty to preserve a proper balance between the two. This involves protection against arbitrary seizures and assures the individual that the spot of earth which he tends and protects will not be taken from him unless a definitely superior social claim arises and then only with adequate compensation. It is use and occupancy, however, that are important—not abstract legal title. We have often made a fetish of title and have neglected to build a set of principles governing occupancy. One of the greatest contributions to be made by religion to the solution of the land problem is the defining of reciprocal rights and duties of those who own and those who occupy land.

At the base of many difficulties regarding land tenure are imperfect human relations. The Christian plea for justice "man to man" should be directed to all interests: (1) owner, (2) tenant (including the farm laborer), and (3) the consumer of farm products. Certain obligations rest upon all of these groups. All occupants, for example, should love the land. Only those who love it can properly conserve and use it, and only those who love it should live upon it.

The owner, if he be guided by Christian principles, will not want too much land. Whether a given amount is too much depends upon his ability to administer it for the welfare of those who work upon it as well as for his own profit. No formula is available for determining how many acres are too much. It will vary for different types of farming. The skill of the owner as an administrator is a large factor. Some owners can efficiently manage a larger number of acres than others. This is an unexplored field for Christian ethics, although the general teachings on the subject of acquisitiveness should certainly apply. We have only lately come to recognize that land speculation is immoral. The amount of tillable land is limited; the managerial skill of men is limited. These two facts add up to the desirability of having a standard as to the size of holdings so that management and the extent of holdings are brought into proper correlation.

. . . Farm labor has a greater stake in management than it has generally recognized. Those of us who emphasize human needs sometimes fail to appreciate this. As the laborer is worthy of his hire, so the manager is worthy of *his* hire. The trouble is that management has gotten all mixed up with high finance, and when that happens, exploitation of farm workers follows. Generally it is the capital charge and not the management fee that takes an inordinate share of the farm returns. The resident owner-manager who accepts his ownership as a social charge will adopt generous policies toward his workers and tenants, but this is hardly possible for the manager who is under pressure to show a big dividend for the absentee owners.

. . . This comment on the superiority of resident management over absenteeism will not be construed, I hope, as an apologia for the tenancy system as now operated. No indictments of that system, however, should be predicated on the assumption that landowners as a class are devoid of human kindness. To the extent that personal factors enter into the equation, the fault is inherent in human nature itself. We are all too unyielding in our thinking when vested interests are involved. However, support may be found for land reforms in the landed group itself. The Duke of Richmond contributed much to the nineteenth-century reforms in England, and it is not impossible for the same progressiveness to be developed among individual owners in this country, although as a class they will oppose change.

An important rule for the owner in developing a Christian standard is to divide the profits of the land equitably with renters and workers. The question arises, why not leave such matters to the law of economics? Economic law does not work in this case for the reason that tenants have no bargaining power. A surplus farm population depresses farm wages just as surplus commodities depress prices. (This is, of course, not the only factor in the low wage situations on farms.) Unless ethical considerations are invoked, standards will continue to be low and injustices will be tolerated.

. . . Finally, the owner as the dominant partner in the land relationship should respect the renter. This involves a quality that lies outside the economic sphere, one that requires a recognition of the worth of the tenant as a person. The owner may wish to terminate the arrangement as soon as he can legally do so; he may feel that he has been deprived of his rights as an owner, but the Christian standard implies something more fundamental than these strict legal and economic considerations. On the part of both owner and renter, it often requires patience and forbearance. It is not something one can acquire quickly—it comes like other Christian graces with practice. Something very valuable in human relations is lacking when a land tenure relationship rests wholly on economic interests. For example, the share-crop arrangement, as the South knows it, represents a deterioration. Whatever the reason for the change, the original idea of a partnership in which one furnished land and the other his labor has ceased to be a partnership based on confidence and has become an employment, unfortunately accompanied by distrust in many cases.

. . . The Christian attitude was stated by Paul as the basis for a practical and just relationship—"The husbandman that laboreth must be the first to partake of the fruits"—not all the fruits but the first fruits and evidently a sufficient share of them. If this simple principle could be established as a universal working rule for farm operations, many unchristian attitudes would disappear.

The Christian's relation to land also embraces obligations on the part of the tenant and farm worker. There is first the same duty to conserve the soil that rests upon the owner and the further duty to the owner to protect the improvements. This is not easy, for one-third of our nearly three million tenants move every year. It requires a moral sense to impose the restraints that are necessary to this conservation where the renters' hold on the land is so tenuous. Society's offense on this point is a great one. We who work on the public side of the problem were rebuked by one tenant who said, "Every politician ought to be a tenant for a while. About the third time the dust of an Alabama road settled on his household stuff, he'd decide something ought to be done." To permit a system to exist in which there is no security for the tenant is unpardonable, but the tenant is not relieved thereby from the obligation to avoid abuse to the physical properties.

There are other reciprocal duties on the tenants' part. They revolve around the owners' duty as set out above to respect the tenants. The renter owes the same respect to the owner.

To deserve security, he must seek the confidence and trust that spring out of a regard for the person with whom he deals. He must not suffer the forfeiting of that respect for frivolous reasons, but as a Christian he must seek to place the personal relations of the contract above technical rights.

Finally, what is society's duty? We do not know what the pattern of American farm life will look like when we complete the establishment of an ethical base for its operations. It is a big country and with its varied crops and markets there will be room for various types of farm administration. In general, however, we know that there must be a wider distribution of land and of opportunities in connection with it. The three alternatives seem to be: (1) the family type farm with co-operative ownership of expensive facilities; (2) co-operative leasing or ownership of land as well as facilities; (3) private or corporate ownership of extensive holdings with legally imposed standards of housing, sanitation, and other living conditions. These standards would be achieved by collective bargaining with farm workers, although collective bargaining is never a complete assurance of justice, since some will likely be attached to farm life who cannot come within the protective influences of any economic power. There must be better access to urban markets and finer co-operation between producer and consumer. Consumer chiseling as well as producer profiteering must be outlawed. The agricultural drive for ethical principles is, therefore, bound up in the problem of establishing justice in the entire economic system.

Better Planning for Good Relations

For a long time I have been interested in developing small industries in the agricultural communities of the South, and I hope to see greater efforts in this direction. In the background is the pronounced population shift for the area. Arkansas in the ten-year period, 1940–1950, for example, had a net loss of 39,000 people, but to get the complete picture one must also consider the fact that there was an excess of 280,000 births over deaths so that we had an out-migration in the decade of about a third of a million people. In terms of agricultural stability this was a rather favorable development for it meant a change of farm practices that on the whole is wholesome and economically beneficial. If, however, we had been able to provide employment opportunities for people who migrated to the Northeast and the West Coast, we would have avoided the necessity for some business readjustments in the area that are rather painful. I think that Arkansas is somewhat typical of the South, at least many parts of it.

I believe that the many natural advantages we have for certain types of industrial development should be more fully utilized, but more careful planning by the states and by the Federal Government is essential to a sound program. In the effort to strengthen our own economic situation, we must not contribute to dislocations elsewhere, and we must pursue policies that do not exploit labor or invoke unsound governmental policies, such as certain types of tax exemptions and other artificial encouragements to industry.

The South's awakened interest in this problem receives attention in other areas, particularly in New England, but the

NOTE: From the *Journal of Public Law*, Emory University Law School, Georgia, Vol. 2, No. 1, Spring, 1953.

reaction is often emotional, and one of our basic difficulties is in securing an acceptance by industrial leaders elsewhere of certain over-all national aspects of the problem. It is difficult for business and political leaders elsewhere to concede one basic principle: that the South is entitled to a wage differential. I am just as sure, however, that we must be clear on the point that the differential must not be so pronounced as to tend toward exploitation, and certainly it must not be based upon a denial of collective bargaining and other rights of the workers. We must exert ourselves in this transition period to embrace policies that are fair to both management and labor, as well as the public.

In the achievement of these aims, it is important to have informal conversations between leaders who are anxious to base a national policy on the elements of good will and mutual progress. Such discussions, open and full, would do much to reconcile some of the existing conflicts between the various regions of the nation. This discussion plan would also do much to further belief in the efficacy of small industries in the towns and villages, and would encourage the development of a national policy movement without hurting the cities or taking away from established communities the gains that they have been able to make in the past.

II *From Politician to Congressman*

Two unsuccessful races for governor and one race for Congress, in which he was counted out by a patent fraud, showed Brooks Hays the seamy side of politics and taught him the lessons of defeat. After serious canvass of the desirability of withdrawal from public life in 1942, he determined on a further congressional race. Since then, he has represented Arkansas's Fifth District for eight terms, entering into the political process with humor, tolerance, and understanding.

❖

Should I Stay in Politics?

It was a hot afternoon in late July, 1928, and I had paused to wipe the sweat from my face during a political speech at Big Flat, Arkansas, in the heart of the Ozarks, when a husky listener suddenly spoke up, "That talk about taxation is all right, I reckon, but what we folks up here want to know is, How do you stand on this here evolution bill?" I was telling the voters of that village why I should be elected governor of Arkansas. It was my first race for a public office and I was less than thirty years old.

At that age running for state office is a great adventure! For weeks before the speaking engagements there were interesting conferences on strategy and the preliminary cam-

NOTE: Unpublished reflections written in 1936.

43

paigning (shaking hands with everyone in the towns and hailing the farmers in the fields)—a lot of fun if you enjoy that sort of thing, and I do. The campaign was hard. I made five to nine full-length speeches a day with no loud-speaker and chalked up a record of 303 speeches (or as someone said, one speech 303 times) for the season. I finished at Little Rock with an audience of about 15,000 which was said to be the largest political gathering in the state's history. (But Huey Long put me in the shade four years later at the same place with a crowd twice as big.)

We take our politics seriously in Arkansas. Babies named for me that year are going to school now and occasionally I hear from one of them. In Boone County one youngster said, "Mr. Hays, you gotta win. I've named my calf for you, and he's in the calf show a week after the election. If you lose I'm afriad he'll lose, too." Poor boy! He didn't know how *often* I was destined to lose. I spoke in schoolhouses, in brush arbors, in blacksmith shops, and in the open. I slept sitting bolt upright in the car between appointments. I ate sandwiches between speeches, and once I changed clothes in the back of the car while being driven from one town to the next. While speaking in a brush arbor in south Arkansas, one day I suddenly found my audience convulsed with laughter, and I thought I had said the wrong thing until I glanced around and saw a large rooster on the table by me drinking out of the glass which the chairman had provided.

I sought out-of-the-way places. In one remote community I heard a resident say, "Well, he's the first candidate for governor that ever spoke in our place." But his neighbor said, "Nope, they wuz a fellow through here in 1898." The introductions were interesting. I liked best the occasional reference, "The cheerful crusader." At one town, a morning appointment, while waiting for the meeting to open, I engaged the chairman in conversation. He was about eighty years of age, I judged, and was very cordial. I warmed to him. I thought, "I'll get a grand introduction here. The old man is mellow, he's interested in young men, and he'll talk about the aspirations of youth." I was basking in the contemplation of it when the old man arose and said, "Fellow citizens, we got a candidate for governor here this morning. I ain't for him, I think he's too young for the office, but I hope you give the boy a good hearing." I got it!

. . . Early in 1924 a petition urging me to run for prosecuting attorney was laid on my desk, and I was about ready to announce when the brother of a fellow townsman, who wanted the office badly, interceded, "Please don't run against Bud"; so I melted, stepped out of the political picture, and went to the mountains with my wife and year-old daughter for a vacation. While I was on that vacation, just thirty days before the 1924 primary, I was called to Little Rock to manage the campaign of a lawyer twice my age for attorney general of the state. He was elected and I became the assistant in charge of civil law litigation. For two years I had a hectic time defending state officials. A temperamental governor provoked some interesting litigation, and thanks to him and a close friend who handled the publicity I found myself a "state figure."

I wanted to run for attorney general in 1928, but one of my fellow assistants, an older man and a close friend, wanted to run and I melted again. I simply couldn't step in the way of his plans. Again I thought, "I'm out of politics for a while." But suddenly in February of 1928 Governor John E. Martineau, in his first term, resigned to accept an appointment to the Federal bench, leaving an open field for the governor's office. I announced my candidacy because a lot of influential young leaders thought I could win, and I was sure I wouldn't be permanently damaged if I lost. The lieutenant governor, who automatically stepped into the governor's office, became a candidate and, with his opposition divided among six opponents, won the nomination. I was the runner-up.

. . . When I lost again in 1930, my family took our reverses without complaint. Don't let anyone tell you that the only women who contribute to political movements are those who accept committee and club assignments. What about the wives and mothers of the casualties of political warfare? I believe they will get an extra star or two in the heavenly crown. Curtailed income required adjustments that were made with great difficulty, and it would serve no good purpose to detail the measures that the Hays family adopted. I did manage to organize some public speaking classes for businessmen, and we lived on the tuition from those who were so fired with ambition to speak that they were willing to trust themselves to me.

For a good part of my life election years have been like oases, and the 1932 campaign opened with my name still before the public as a potential winner. Hopes revived. "The old horse has a lot of life in him yet," they said. But one of my friends decided to run for governor; so I stepped aside for him. Just before the ticket closed, I filed for Democratic national committeeman (chosen by primary in our state) and though I made no campaign was elected over a strong candidate. The victory was obviously a result of my two races for governor. With the defeat of my friend for the governor's office I found that the committeeman's job (no salary) was the only thing we had saved from the wreckage of a five year's crusade.

. . . Then came the hectic campaign for Congress to fill a vacancy that arose. The 1933 legislature had finally adopted the run-off primary plan which I had advocated for several years. With three of us in the race it was apparent that a run-off would be necessary. In the first primary I led the nearest candidate by 1,600 votes, but the two candidates combined on me in the run-off. It was a bitter fight. I feel quite sure I was the rightful nominee but the central committee certified my opponent.

. . . My close friends were crushed by this third defeat within five years. I wondered what I could do. The law practice was gone; my partner had been forced to seek a federal position and had gone to Washington as a Treasury Department official. I was completely "busted." One afternoon shortly after the court decision my telephone rang, and the operator said, "Washington City is calling." I heard her say, "Go ahead, Miss Perkins." I nearly fell out of the ninth-story window. Then I heard the Secretary of Labor, "Mr. Hays, I am calling to ask if you will accept a position in the state NRA office which we are preparing to set up." Would I accept? Miss Perkins will never know why I stuttered so. I don't stutter often. I was delirious, that's all. I accepted.

I served a year with NRA and in 1935 Dr. Tugwell asked me to become one of his assistants. Here I am now trying to do my part in the Resettlement program, having the time of my life doing it.

. . . I am interested in correcting the injustices in the economic order, particularly in the South, and I am willing to assume a responsibility for protests. But protesters aren't always vote-getters. Furthermore, I believe in progress through the democratic process rather than in the spectacular schemes of political opportunists.

Obviously, politics for me will never be a bed of roses. There is the question of finances, always a serious one for those of us who get into the game without a private fortune at our command. Another element is the consideration one has for his friends. In my case, after three defeats I don't want to ask them to get into another fight unless there is reasonable assurance of victory. What to do about the future is, therefore, not a simple question. Sometimes an ambitious youngster asks me for advice about *his* future—should he go into politics? I used to say, "Sure"; now I never give a categorical answer.

Still, I think I'll stay with it. When I look at one side of the ledger I find a lot to my credit for the ten years activity. I am acquainted with people in every township in Arkansas and am generally considered "respectable." Some of the older politicians call me an upstart; the conservatives think I'm a little wild; but thousands of friends will start with me if I make another race. Should I stay in politics? I wish I knew the answer!

❖

Lincoln and the South

Mr. Hays of Arkansas. Mr. Speaker, the memory of no other man has had the unifying influence for this Nation as that of Abraham Lincoln. There are many things for the South to recall in tenderness and appreciation, but the utterances and actions of no others arrayed against us in 1861–65 compare with those of the man who "though the leader against her in war can never be justly said to have been her enemy." These were the words of J. G. de R. Hamilton of the University of North Carolina in 1915.

. . . The sources of the South's feeling are found in the great human qualities of Lincoln. When others misunder-

Note: *Congressional Record*, Extension of Remarks, House of Representatives, February 15, 1944.

stood the South, he seemed to know the mind and purpose of our people. When others expected humiliating admissions of error which the South could not give, he asked only that we take our place as restored and honored members of the Union. To Mr. Adams in 1861 he gave instructions "not to indulge in expressions of harshness or disrespect or even impatience concerning the seceding States, their agents, or their people" and further to remember that the people of the South "throughout all political misunderstandings and alienations, still are and always must be our kindred and countrymen."

. . . Lincoln's democracy, his simplicity, his appreciation of the common man—these were qualities which found a response in our hearts. In reverencing the memory of Lincoln we would not detract from the possessive feeling which is rightfully the North's, and our pride is sufficiently served in recalling that he lived during the first impressionable years under Southern skies and that he spoke feelingly of his Southern heritage.

The South does not question that Lincoln shared our suffering in the war. To his friend, George P. Floyd, the hotel keeper at Quincy, Illinois, he said: "I have not suffered by the South, I have suffered with the South. Their pain has been my pain. Their loss has been my loss. What they have gained, I have gained."

This was one of the deep and moving sentiments of his nature and partially accounts for the high place he holds in the affections of the South.

Such a life helps us to pierce the mystery contained in the beautiful lines of St. John: "And the Word was made flesh, and dwelt among us." Many of us carry the impressions gained in boyhood from those who could speak from personal memory of the work of this great man. From their accounts as from the pages of recorded history we conclude that the idea of human sympathy and limitless good will for a little while became flesh and dwelt among us.

❖

Diary of Congressional Visit to Europe

When Congressman Judd and I took off in the palatial flying boat of the British Airways on September 2, I hadn't been so excited since Ringling Brothers came to Russellville in 1911. We occupied "the tail cabin," which was as large as some hotel rooms I have seen. The first night we flew to a North Atlantic base and the second lap required just 13½ hours to get us into the harbor of Foynes, in Ireland. ("Eire" it is to Mr. DeValera, who is so insistent on the use of his mother tongue that nearly all of the signs we saw were printed in both Gaelic and English.)

To get from Foynes to an interior air field, we rode in a chartered bus for forty miles through County Limerick and other historic localities. I must give Hollywood credit for having faithfully reproduced the Irish villages and the countryside for when we stopped for two hours at the village Adare to wait on another bus, I found on the streets and in the shops people who seemed to have walked right off of a movie set. There was the peasant riding on a two-wheel cart, urging on a plodding donkey, and beside him was his family coming in for the ride or for marketing on a small scale. It would have agonized an American milk inspector to see the driver of a milk cart take the bucket tendered by the prospective purchaser and lower it into the can and immerse it completely, drawing a dripping full pail for the lady.

NOTE: Unpublished report of a trip made in September, 1944.

. . . The last lap of the trip was in a land plane, completely blacked-out (a concession to Eire), and we landed near London in a driving rain—I had expected only a fog. In a little while it was clear, and we drove with a British colonel to our hotel, The Dorchester, adjoining Hyde Park.

London covers a tremendous space—perhaps thirty miles across—and we drove through several areas where the air raids and the robot bombs had done their worst damage. The destruction is appalling. The Government recently revealed that more than a million homes had been damaged, perhaps a fifth completely destroyed, but to me the amazing thing is that so many buildings remain undamaged. As one man said, "You can see that the Jerries missed more plyces than they hit."

It was late in the afternoon when we registered but we did not wait to eat. We wanted to see the Parliament buildings and Westminster Abbey so we started out without a map or guide. Suddenly we came upon an imposing building. What is it, I asked, and the guard disgustedly said, "Buckingham Palace"; so I will never say anything again about the two ladies who stopped me in front of our Capitol one day to ask, "What can this building be?"

Near Buckingham Palace we saw the terrible damage to the barracks and the chapel used by British troops. Even Westminster Abbey suffered slightly from bomb damage. We had been told to carry our flashlights (or "torches" as the British say), but we had not realized how badly we would need them. The London blackout is no sham. The city is utterly and completely blacked out. Obstructions in the street have a slight illumination and the taxis have a gleam of light —that is all. It gave us a queer sensation to feel our way back to the hotel and then suddenly to enter a fully lighted lobby with people coming and going in a normal way. One of the things I look forward to is seeing Washington with its usual night lights.

The spirit of the people of Britain is magnificent. They have suffered—really beyond the power of visitors to describe —but they have an amazing ability to take it without complaint and to go about their work without allowing their irritations to show. Underneath the calm exterior, however, I think that there is a feeling of righteous wrath that such barbarities should have been practiced. They have been affected by the flying bombs more than reports have indicated. It might have been an effective weapon if used earlier in the war, but now the most obvious result is the added determination that Germany shall not be permitted to construct such instruments of death again.

A few of the flying bombs came over while we were there. They are terrifying things. The alarm system works well, and I was aroused by the sirens after midnight several times and once I was sure that the bomb was flying close to the hotel. I knew the danger to us had passed only when I heard a loud explosion a few blocks away, but I knew too that it meant death for others.

. . . One of our first visits was with the American ambassador—the modest but interesting "Republican" from New Hampshire, Mr. Winant. I had been with him on one or two occasions in America and had been fascinated by his quiet manner and profound philosophy. One time I had heard him say in a dinner conversation that a man's life should be full of intelligent and energetic action but that the chief quality of life is "devoted self-sacrifice." I recommend that to anyone who might be surrendering hope that modern politicians can cultivate ideals.

The Foreign Secretary, Mr. Eden, was a guest at Mr. Winant's luncheon and we liked him. Unfortunately, Mr.

Judd and I had to leave early for an engagement with Mr. Eden's Parliamentary Secretary, Mr. George Hall, a Welshman with twenty-three years experience in the House of Commons. He was a coal miner until he was past forty—"was in the pits when elected to Parliament," as he phrased it—and today still calls himself a Socialist (along with most members of the Labour Party) though a loyal member of "The Government" and a supporter of coalition policies.

The Parliament buildings appear to be one structure but in reality represent a gradual process of construction, dating back several centuries to Norman days. The room where the Commons now meet is the permanent home of the House of Lords and is just a little smaller than the larger body is used to, though I was surprised to learn that the regular meeting place seats less than 500 (there are 619 members). Strangely enough, they do not intend to do anything about it when improvements are made in the building. And they like the arrangement which requires the opposing parties to face each other in formal sessions.

We had an opportunity later to see how the House of Commons functions, having seats in the gallery at the opening on September 26. We had expected only short formalities and quick adjournment but found quite a lot of business to be conducted, including a personal appearance of Mr. Churchill who answered a number of questions from critical members. Our own Congress has nothing resembling the questioning of the ministers, and I was convinced from observing the practice that the Kefauver plan proposing an adaptation of the English method to our House of Representatives has real merit.

Before going into the gallery, we stood in the lobby for the procession led by the Speaker with his wig and robe with a trainbearer in knee breeches and a sword, and we stood uncovered when the guard shouted, "Hats off, strangers," which applies to everyone, including the guard himself. At the end of the session the guard calls out, "Who goes home?"—the signal that the session has ended and a reminder that one day it was not safe to travel alone in certain parts of London, and the guards arranged to organize the members in groups to proceed together to their homes.

. . . One day we rode to a bomber base in North England, arriving just before a mission of a hundred planes returned. The general in charge took us into "the tower" to see something of the mechanics of communication and the operating plans for getting the planes into formation and back to the landing field in safety. When we went into the room there was an obvious anxiety and tension, which we were told is always evident when the planes are coming in. The ambulances were at their stations, and the chaplain walked back and forth in front of them, waiting to see if there were wounded. A major identified him. "A fine lot of men," he said. The ground crew gazed nervously at the flecks in the sky. The officer near us counted the planes. "Two missing," he said, "but maybe they're safe." He called to one of his staff, "Check with the captain." In a moment he was told that the missing pilots had telephoned from France that they had made forced landings but were all right.

Although we ate with the officers, the fare is substantially the same for all of the troops, and it was excellent. None of the men I talked with during the entire trip had serious complaints to make of the food, except on the boats, and after our week of the civilian diet it looked wonderful to us. The civilians of England have had a tough time getting enough to eat, or rather I should say, in providing sufficient variety. There were generally plenty of potatoes, and in season there were green vegetables from their victory gardens. (There were vegetable crops everywhere—even in the spacious parks which are the boast of London.) Still, I often left the table just a little hungry; so we grabbed at every chance to eat with our troops. There are rationed articles in the camps such as gum and chocolate, and I was glad I took a box of candy bars to pass out to my Arkansas visitors. Civilians have almost forgotten what oranges look like, and I saved two, given me by an officer, to serve an English friend at breakfast the morning I left London. He said it was the first he had tasted in months.

On the whole the English farmers have done a grand job of stepping up food production. They are quick to give credit to the United States, however, for the farm machinery and fertilizer without which their marvelous record would not have been possible. Their achievements were based upon maximum use of their land resources—a policy they had not forced themselves to adopt before the war. I have the figures of the Minister of Agriculture on last year's production, and they are impressive. The officials thought first of a 15 per cent increase over the previous years but finally fixed it at 30 per cent and were gratified to get an 80 per cent increase in most of the essential crops.

. . . The city of Dover on the English Channel is entitled to a large place in the history of this war. We spent Wednesday of our first week there, and it proved to be one of our most exciting days. Since 1940 there have been more than 3,000 alarms in Dover, an average of three a day. We could see the Calais coast where the German guns were placed— high chalk cliffs like the one on which we stood.

The old castle from which we watched the American boats in the channel is nearly a thousand years old—one of the first erected by the Normans. We spent the morning examining the castle walls and grounds, all of which are splendidly preserved, and while we were finishing a simple lunch which closed with "a sweet or a savory," meaning sponge cake with custard sauce or a piece of cheese (take your choice), the alarm rang, and the loud-speaker signaled to the people to go to the shelters. An official of the Ministry of Information was with us and with obvious sarcasm he said, "Just look at the people panic." (The Germans had spoken of "the panics at Dover.") They were walking slowly and unperturbedly to the shelters.

"Do you want to go to the shelter," the guide asked, "or shall we stay out and see something?" I was curious but not heroic so I let Judd decide. "Let's stay above ground," he said and I agreed. In a moment I saw two bright flashes on the German side. The guard said, "In seventy-eight seconds something will happen." And it did. A few hundred yards below us two terrific blasts took place. (If I should say as I did in London later, "a few yards from us," it will be inadvertant— though my colleagues vow that when I get through with this story in Arkansas it will be gory.) We hurried to the scene. Two buildings had been demolished but the casualties were slight. Four people were hurt—only one of them seriously.

We went to the first-aid station and saw how these fine people give medical aid to their casualties; then we went to the shelters. The chalk cliffs are ideal for this purpose. In the great tunnels which have been drilled below are adequate facilities required for housing and feeding the people in emergencies. But it is not a comfortable place. I wondered how the women, for example, managed to endure the long hours with only knitting and conversation to engage them. Sometimes darkness would make the knitting impossible, and I should think they would have run out of something to say after the first year. But one could never tell from their expressions that they were tired. They are endowed with a remarkable patience.

The brief bombardment we saw was among the last, and we were still in England when "the expiring monster on the other side coughed up his last missiles," as the newspaper referred to it. The people of Dover who had stood this long siege with such tenacity and good temper could then come out of the chalk caves for good. All of England has given Dover unstinted praise and were happy with them when their shelling ended.

. . . With such a history Britain seems to me to have a certain grandeur in the smoke stains and the ugly gaps where the bombs have struck, but the many apologies for London's physical condition was proof that the people were proud of its peacetime appearance. The British are given to making apologies for imperfections anyway. They seemed to fear that we would hold even the occasional bad weather against the Empire. You don't have to be in England long to perceive that the Empire represents far more than a political entity— it is a concept around which deep affections and loyalties have been built.

. . . In Winchester, south of London, I saw attractive gift shops, but our schedule was such that we had to take our choice between shopping or seeing England's oldest cathedral, the famous one which was started shortly after William the Conqueror established his headquarters in that neighborhood. It was completed in 1170, and it is larger and more inspiring than any church structure I have seen in our country, although the National Cathedral at Washington will, when completed, exceed it in size. Charles Wesley was the organist at this place for thirteen years and composed some of his great hymns at Winchester.

The story of England's cathedrals and church buildings is a very interesting one, especially since the blitz has damaged so many of the prominent ones.

The Government is prepared to bear the expense of rebuilding all wrecked church buildings, both the established and free churches, though this aid will not extend to furnishings. When I asked some of the free church leaders if help of American churches would be requested, it was indicated that aid along other lines would be more urgently needed and that the rehabilitation of Christian churches on the continent would have priority. A gift of $15,000.00 which American Baptists had just sent to Baptists in Britain will be used to aid individuals who have suffered most severely from the bomb damage.

The great thrill of the trip came when General John C. H. Lee, who has distinguished himself as head of the Communications Division, sent word to us that General Eisenhower had approved our request for permission to visit Normandy and Paris. At the same time, the General invited us to have lunch with him at Headquarters. We used air transportation for the trip and spent the busiest three days of the trip on the soil of France.

It was late in the evening when we reached the place where the invasion began, but there was time to take a look at this historic spot. We had a more comprehensive view of the terrain next morning and also of the continuing activities of our supply organization. I shall not try to describe their mammoth operation. Even while I looked on, as vast amounts of food and ammunition moved past us, I could not comprehend what it meant in terms of military power. The secret statistics given us in Paris on the subject had little meaning for those of us not accustomed to seeing large armies moved and fed.

The experience to be longest remembered was the view of the narrow beaches where our men held on for the first terrible hours of the invasion. After seeing that landscape and hearing the eyewitness account from the officers who guided us, I will never be lacking in appreciation of what our men accomplished on D-Day and in the bitter fighting for Normandy. Colonel Talley, of the Engineers, took us over fields not yet cleared of mines, cautiously leading us where he knew none were planted and from the high ground above the narrow beach described the advantage held by the Germans that first morning. The hills are high and steep and the pillboxes were skilfully placed. We examined some of them. Except for the precision bombing of our air forces it would have been literally impossible to pierce that kind of defense. The Germans have developed marvelous skill in concrete construction, and the walls, some of which were three and four feet thick, were amply reinforced with steel. Yet our bombs tore many of them apart.

. . . Now here we were—twelve Congressmen—solemnly looking at the place where our men had heroically begun the destruction of Fortress Europa. In clear view was the cemetery near Colleville, where thousands of those lads are buried, and our own flag floated from a high pole in the center. It was hallowed soil and everyone of us felt very reverent then, but we didn't say anything about it because the sentiment was deep and defied expression. Later in the day we visited another cemetery at Le Cande, on the road to Cherbourg where 4,000 of our men are buried, and we went inside and looked at the seemingly endless rows of white crosses with here and there a Star of David—all of them Americans. No distinction was made as to rank. We paused a moment beside Lieutenant General McNair's grave, which was marked like the others. There were flowers lying on some of the carefully tended graves and the guard said that almost every day unknown French women walked into the cemetery and dropped the fresh bouquets.

. . . In Normandy we visited a field hospital where we saw

how our doctors and nurses are giving marvelous service to the wounded men under extreme conditions. We were surprised to find in the tents practically the same modern operating and laboratory equipment that we found in the base hospitals and the staff carried on just as if they were living normal lives. We found civilians there, too—some of the French having been wounded in the fighting and they were receiving the same care and attention.

Three children, Jeanne, Andre, and Marcel, were in one tent, and the nurse told us that she suspected the Germans of deliberately setting fire to the home where they were burned. American dolls were lying on the beds, and I assumed we had again come upon the trail of the Red Cross.

. . . General Eisenhower received us at his headquarters on September 22, and we had a grand two-hour luncheon session with him—very informal and unofficial, asking no embarrassing questions about strategy or "when will the war be over." Even if his schedule contains a notation "the war ends here," no one could be sure that generals like Bradley, Hodges, Patton, Simpson, Clark, and Smith or Montgomery and Alexander, on the British side, wouldn't move it up on him.

In London we picked up several stories about Montgomery, who just naturally becomes the subject of legends; Churchill is said to have remarked about him: "In defeat indomitable, in advance invincible, in victory insufferable."

Our group was greatly impressed by General Eisenhower's easy manner and obvious grasp of his tremendous responsibilities. It was an inspiring session for all of us and we reluctantly pulled ourselves away so he could go back to his work.

. . . The rest of our stay in England was uneventful. There were a few more rather formal social events which had some value because we were given an opportunity to meet and talk

with a number of British officials and journalists, but there
was a feeling of anticlimax after the trip to France and we
were ready to start home.

We were glad to learn, however, that we were to embark at
a port in Scotland and our hosts arranged for us to visit Belfast, Glasgow, Edinburgh, and the lake country north of
Glasgow before our boat left.

In Belfast the Lord Mayor and the Prime Minister of
Northern Ireland entertained us in great fashion and arranged
for us to see something of the charm of rural Ulster, as well
as their important industries, shipbuilding, linen, and manu-
facturing. It is easy to understand after seeing the country and
talking to the people why the northern counties feel more
congenial with England and Scotland than with the rest of
Ireland. Ulster was settled by Scots and bears the impress of
their culture and political ideas. It was surprising to find so
much information among Ulsterites regarding our own country and so much interest in our affairs. At the Prime Minister's
dinner I sat next to a lawyer who embarrassed me by display-
ing a greater knowledge than I possessed of the movements of
their Presbyterian emigrants in the Southern states. He knew
that the South Irish emigrants had gone north and the North
Irish had gone south when they came to America and described the political significance of developments in America.

In Scotland we were fascinated by the two great cities:
Glasgow the industrial center and Edinburgh the city of culture and historic interest. And our day in the Loch Lomond
neighborhood will never be forgotten. Five and a half million
people live in an area only two-thirds the size of Arkansas
and they live pretty well, if we could judge from a brief survey.
The cottages of the farmers are well constructed—too well,
said one of our hosts. They built for future generations, and
the thick solid walls cause considerable dampness, but I think

nature just made Scotland a damp country. With 30 per cent greater rainfall than we have (and evenly distributed, too) they are able to keep the fields green and productive most of the year.

They are accomplishing a transition in agriculture that will give their farmers and tenants greater security and, in some cases, larger holdings. Sixty per cent of their farmers have less than sixty acres and only a third hold title to their land, but tenancy and small units have not defeated the development of a sound and fairly prosperous agriculture. Tenancy is preferred by most farmers. I talked to one whose family had had continuous occupancy of the farm for fifty-six years, and he had not seen the owner in a number of years, but he wanted to remain a tenant. The leases average fourteen years and tenants are protected by law against arbitrary removal and can secure compensation for improvements, some of which do not require the owner's consent. Both renters and owners seem pleased with the tenure arrangements.

One of the high points in our trip was the evening with Sir Harry Lauder. He was only seventy-four and in excellent health. He invited us to "high tea" but it looked like supper to us, and we were in his "bonnie wee home" (it wasn't so wee) from four until after nine. If you remember his songs and stories from the last war, you know we had a good time. I was shocked into realizing that a generation has passed when I found a blank expression on my son's and daughter's faces at the mention of Harry Lauder but great excitement when I said that Bing Crosby returned on the same boat. When Sir Harry saw me looking interestedly at a stained glass window at the stair landing inscribed, "This House Is God's Gift," he said, "I put it that way because it was built with the money I made from singing and acting, and you see those talents were given to me."

I felt real proud of myself to be the only one of the group who remembered "Roamin' in the Gloamin'" well enough to sing it with him, and while it won't lead to any professional offers, my voice didn't crack and he seemed to think well of our duet. Then he sang "The Laddies Who Fought and Won"—seated in a comfortable chair with his short legs stretched out in front of him. Adding to the color were his kilts, and the gay stockings knitted by his niece, Miss Greta Lauder—a grand hostess—who maintains his home for him since his wife's death a few years ago. He remembers many incidents of his American trips and mentioned Little Rock and Texarkana where he was given a watch—"standing on the state line with one foot in Arkansas and one in Texas."

He does a lot of entertaining for our men and only a few days before our visit had been to Prestwick, near Glasgow for a performance in an American hospital. "Don't let the mothers worry about the medical treatment," he said. "While I was singing, I saw men—just returned from France—being assigned to beds. I went into every ward and know the treatment is of the very finest type. Later I saw some of them lifted into planes to go back to their homes in America."

The great man promised that having already made a number of farewell tours of America, he might want to make one or two more after the war. That would be something to look forward to.

. . . The praise of America's part in the war which we heard on every hand convinced us that the gratitude of the people knows no bounds, and having come in such close contact with their sacrifices, we were able to speak feelingly of our appreciation of their part in the supreme fight to save our civilization. . . .

Campaign Year: 1948

This year, I'm sitting pretty. Most of my colleagues in the House of Representatives are all hot and bothered: here they are at the nation's capital, while the men who are running against them for the very seats they so unwillingly continue to sit on are stirring round their district, making friends, influencing people, admiring livestock, and eating chicken dinners.

I'm hot, all right—who in Washington isn't? But I'm not bothered. This year, I didn't have opposition. In the Fifth District of Arkansas, when we say opposition we mean Democratic opposition in the primary. There is a Republican running in the election in November, but I believe he won't hold it against me if I say I'm not bothered.

So I can watch the other boys sweat it out, and I can sit in the shade and say that campaigning is the breath of life in a democracy without getting as out of breath as I sometimes have been, without vigorous opponents breathing down the back of my neck or equally vigorous friends giving me the kiss of death in front of everybody.

The sheriff of Yell County was exactly right. When someone asked him whether he'd rather run without an opponent or with one, he said, "I'd a lot rather be unopposed. The other way, I have to laugh so often when I ain't tickled."

Don't let anyone tell you, though, that running without opposition is all gravy. When you speak at the community picnic, you may not have an opponent to compete for the folks' attention, but there's almost always a good dogfight or two, and the merry-go-rounds and the swings pull away your listeners and make them squeal when they get there. It's sur-

NOTE: Unpublished reflections written in 1948.

prising, too, how many firecrackers are left over from the Glorious Fourth—all summer!

. . . I managed to stop short of the mistake made by one of our other candidates for state office. During the hand-shaking phase of his campaign he bought tickets from one town to another, without caring particularly where he was or working under any set schedule. One day when he was handing out his cards in a little town, his prospect said, "Yes, sir. That's fine and I wish you luck. But you see, we don't vote for that office here." "Oh, yes, you do," my friend replied firmly. "This isn't any little county office. This is a state office, so everybody in the state can vote for it." "I know," the prospect persisted, "but not everybody in the United States. You're in Wister, Oklahoma."

But this year, I not only don't have to go around shaking hands, I don't have to go around remembering people. It's wonderful the pleasure voters take in coming up and looking you in the eye and saying, "You don't remember me." A friend of mine once said it's too bad Mississippi and Oklahoma don't have race tracks and liquor stores; maybe they would draw off some of the meanness that works its way into politics. But Arkansas has both and it doesn't work out like that. The meanness of people who put you on the spot to tell them their names seems to be pretty much everywhere, and don't let any candidate tell you it hasn't given him some bad moments. Like the time I was introduced to a Mrs. Thompson. When it was perfectly clear that I didn't recognize Mrs. Thompson, my friend tried to give me a clue: "You remember Jim Thompson?" I did: "So you're Jim Thompson's mother?" I never saw an expression change so fast, and the change wasn't for the better. "No, I'm Jim Thompson's *wife!*" I got out of that one, though; quickly I said, "Oh, then it's another Jim Thompson; the Jim I'm thinking about is a high-school boy—he was in the headquarters this morning. He isn't married."

It takes quite a man to face this problem squarely, and there aren't many who dare handle it the way Senator Joe Robinson once did when I was in his company. Someone came up with the old story: "You don't know who I am, do you?" The Senator scowled: "No. And now you tell me why the heck I should."

. . . This summer I won't have to sit on platform after platform listening to somebody tell the folks who I am. Every candidate gets a variety of introductions, good, bad, indifferent—and unique. I wish there were more people like the old man at Hindsville who referred to me as that "brilliant young paragon of democracy, the hope of our people." Of course, people don't always say exactly what they mean, or at least it's comforting to hope so. For instance: "Fellow voters, I want to tell you that Jefferson County, the State of Arkansas, the whole United States, are not big enough to hold this man's disability."

This summer my ancestors can rest in peace. I'm downright proud of the fact that I never have pretended to be born on a farm—though I am inclined to reduce the population of the town where I was born until the fields come right up to the main street, and I make a good deal of the time I spent as a boy picking cotton and working in Uncle Will's peach orchard. In fact, I usually mention that it was the feel of peach fuzz on the back of my neck, with the temperature at 105 degrees, that helped me decide to be a statesman and not a farmer.

In the past, I've been attacked as the grandson of a carpetbagger presuming to offer for public office. The date at which Grandfather Hays reached Arkansas, 1879, was a little late to make him a carpetbagger, but it's perfectly true that he was a schoolmate of McKinley's at Allegheny College, and he'd served as a Republican postmaster in Pennsylvania before he started west. My technique has been to admit these things and then get emotional, saying that when my grandparents gathered their few belongings together and came halfway across a continent in response to the warm welcome that had gone out from Arkansas to come and cast lots with our people, they never dreamed that their grandson, fifty years later, would be denied an opportunity to serve the people because of the lateness of their arrival.

Then I switch quickly to Uncle Philip. Grandmother's people have good credentials, and Uncle Philip fought on the right side at Shiloh. By the time I bring him off the battlefield, he's in such bad shape that most good Confederates are hastening to comfort me.

I've had my troubles with financial matters in more recent times. After the session of Congress in which we raised our salaries, I felt called on to do some explaining—upping your own pay while in office is rarely popular. I must have made the point I intended all right, but there was still a catch in it. When questions were called for, a lady rose: "Mr. Hays, I think that was all right. The salary should have been raised. But now that it's up where it ought to be, do you think it will induce better men to run for Congress?"

. . . If taxation has its problems for the candidate, so, in Arkansas and I suspect elsewhere, does religion. One way or another, the religious note does creep into the campaign. There is a politically minded preacher down in Arkansas who works an emotional appeal into his broadcasts and the money pours in. Part of it, he uses to publish religious literature. He claims that "money for the Lord is not subject to the corrupt practices act."

Three days before election, in one of my hotter contests, I reached one of the county seats on a blazing Saturday after-

noon and found a crowd of about 5,000 on hand in the plaza.
My local manager was a prominent Baptist. "Brother ————"
he told me, "is going to open the meeting with prayer."

"Not my meeting," I replied; "let's keep the praying private."

"No use your arguing. There he is at the microphone, just
ready to lead off."

Sure enough, it was too late to do anything about it. But
Brother ————'s prayer turned out to be entirely circumspect.
He asked for a calm spirit and a tolerant attitude; he asked
the Lord to endow everyone with a capacity to discharge his
civic duties in a way becoming to a Christian. He didn't mention my name or ask for success for his candidate. I took over
the meeting feeling all right.

Part way through, I succeeded in relaxing any tension
further; I asked the chairman, who was a prominent Methodist, for a glass of water, and when I handed back the
empty glass, I turned to the audience and said, "That's more
water than I ever found on a Methodist in all my life." Quick
as a flash came his rejoinder: "And I never saw a Baptist
satisfied with so little."

But that wasn't all. When the meeting was over, another
preacher rose to dismiss us with prayer. Where the first one
had asked for patience and tolerance, this brother asked for
the bacon: "O Lord," he cried in a tone that will make Ga-
briel's announcement of the Judgment Day sound feeble,
"send these folks home to work for Brother Brooks and to
put this dear man in Congress to represent our people."

Even though none of my doing, these rousements must
have been effective. A friend of mine asked the leader of the
opposition how the meeting had gone. "Much too well,"
was the answer. "If we're going to carry this county by as
much as fifty votes, we're going to have to steal five hundred

votes from Brooks that we hadn't intended to steal." And that year, I didn't come to Congress.

. . . In some places, the use of money in a campaign is governed by a code. I came right up against this at one county seat when I said, "Uncle Johnny, I hope you're going to turn in a good vote for my friend for governor this time." Uncle Johnny paused. "Well now, Brooks," he said, "I wish I'd uh knowed you was interested in him. It's too late now to help yuh. Purdom Township is going the other way. You see, the other boys sent me a check for $25 and I've cashed it. For me to switch on them now wouldn't be ethical."

. . . But however much doing it takes to get elected, that doing is worthwhile. I used to think that in the long run it didn't make too much difference who held a particular office at any particular time; I used to think that we could survive the errors of judgment of successive candidates if we could prevent the mishandling of the machinery of selecting them. But in times like these, when the margin of national safety is narrow, we must constantly join my lady questioner in a search for ever better men. Otherwise we risk falling for campaign pledges like that of the Arkansas candidate for constable: "Elect me your constable and I won't have no respect for nobody!"

❖

Reflections on the Constituent

We members of Congress have created for our own convenience a mythical character we call the constituent. He is our employer and a very important person. We think of him

NOTE: Unpublished reflections written in 1948.

as the average voter—embodying the composite views of the two or three hundred thousand people whom each of us represents. The fact that there is no such thing as the average man does not interfere with this practice and we are not the only ones who indulge in this fiction. The law has its John Doe, the servicemen their Joe Doakes, and the cartoonists John Q. Citizen.

We assume that this fictional constituent reflects the thinking of our people, but actually we impute to him more of what we hope the people are thinking than objectively we know they think. Nevertheless, it is a helpful device and after every recess I like to appraise the constituent's thinking, also his hopes and his prejudices.

. . . The constituent is confused about the means for reaching some of his goals, but here are four things he wants:

1. He wants peace. He would not say peace at any price, but he thinks Congress and the President ought to be skilful enough to save us from the ruin of an atomic war. At home he wants a more predictable economic system. He doesn't like for the speculators to have so much of the playing field, though he would not disqualify them. He wants prosperity but without the hazards of a boom. He isn't sure about the inflation threat, whether to fear it and encourage bold action to arrest it or to take a chance on getting more than he loses out of the spree. Anyway, he insists that he hasn't the understanding of inflation's total impact to appraise it, and unless he is in the rigidly fixed income class, he is content to just hope things will level off. Pressed for a preference, he will probably say, "Give us more moderate profits with stability." In any event, he does want peace and—if there were any way to have it—a long period of calm. He is tired of crises.

2. When he thinks about the world—the big one which he now vaguely feels himself a part of—he wants it to be a moral

world. He and his neighbor might not agree about what is morally right in given cases, but they would agree that one of the things lacking in our world is an insistence upon moral values at all times and in all places. . . .

3. The third element he desires in his new world is one that he hesitates to speak of. He likes to think he is tough-minded. He does not want the softies to take over. Yet he is sure that more than mathematical justice, more than a cold morality is required. No single word defines this quality. Kindness comes near it. The word "liberalism" as it was once used, before it was associated with an economic cult, would have sufficed. Tolerance would do except that it has a negative ring and is not always a virtue. The constituent knows that we are threatened with a loss of unity. It frightens him when he thinks what France suffered when the same process ran its full course. The Frenchman who thought of his province rather than the republic contributed to France's decline. The tendency of French workers to place the trade union above the nation, and the habits of management to subordinate the general welfare to the exigencies of industrial war conspired to weaken France in her greatest crisis. Having created a grand slogan, "Liberty, Equality, Fraternity," the French made the error of assuming that liberty and equality could be maintained without fraternity. The republic will flourish again only if a way is found to restore their sense of fraternity. . . .

4. The constituent's better nature tells him that some of the tensions of modern life could be eased if he took notice of race problems and exhibited the quality of good will. He is sure that his representative should not entertain for a moment the weird ideas of some of the pressure groups embodied, for example, in FEPC, and he is irritated when the minorities, particularly the Negro group dominated by the non-

South wing, destroy the climate for discussion. Here the representatives must do some straight thinking. Clustered around the concept "representative" are historic values. He represents all of the people, including those who contribute nothing to his election.

. . . The constituent believes, though he may not know he believes, that when the representative ceases to represent all of the people, that day he should be retired from office. And that does not mean he must agree with all groups. That would be impossible since they do not agree with each other, but when he consistently refuses to consider the appeals of any group, even the politically uninfluential, he does violence to the American tradition. . . .

The race question colors the thinking of the constituent. He would be intolerant of his representative's support for those panaceas which have an anti-Southern bias, but he knows that race relations are changing and that alternative solutions must be offered by the Southern white leadership, and participated in by Southern Negro leadership. . . .

And so the mythical man will yearn for peace inside himself—even those who must be exposed to the turmoil of modern life. He will have time for the church if its message is supplying this deep and fundamental need. He may look in vain for the instruments of power for doing in his world that he would like to do, but for the peace within, he will have at hand every aid and facility in the messages of Jesus himself. For Jesus dealt with the strong and elemental forces of human life.

An Essay on Lobbies

Above the entrance to the beautiful building which houses the Department of Justice in Washington are these words: "Justice in the life and administration of the State is possible only as it resides first in the hearts and souls of the people." My nine years of service in the Congress have brought me a deep appreciation of this basic principle in our democracy. There are more than two million employees of the Federal Government, but only 533 are chosen by vote of the people and each voter helps to select only five of this number—the president, the vice-president, his two senators, and a member of the House of Representatives. For that reason we members of Congress must constitute an effective medium for interpreting the people's hopes and purposes to their Government.

The Constitution guarantees to each citizen the right to "petition the Government for a redress of grievance." As a member of the House I can testify that citizens have taken seriously this part of the Bill of Rights. The scores of letters received daily in my office are adequate proof.

It is only when the citizen takes an active interest in his government that we are assured of a sound democracy. The citizen has not only a right but also an obligation to keep a watchful eye on all phases of government. He should not be timid in making known his views to the legislative bodies that make the laws under which he lives—local, state, and national.

. . . What has this to do with the problem of lobbying? In the first place, it shows that the framers of the Constitu-

Note: Unpublished reflections written in 1951.

tion fully intended for the citizen to take a personal and direct interest in his government. The "right of petition" as set forth in the Constitution is the right to lobby. My constituent who demands that I support this bill or oppose that one is engaging in lobbying activity in the purest sense of the word and he is petitioning me, his elected representative, for a redress of what he considers a just grievance.

The demand of the petitioner, obviously, is not always met, but the citizen has the satisfaction of knowing that his point of view has been considered.

Unfortunately, all lobbying is not conducted on this simple, direct basis. In the past generation we have seen develop in all places where government policy is made, organized lobbies who serve only the particular group which they represent. Lobbying has now become a highly complex and often lucrative business open largely to experts.

. . . The writing of legislation has become a highly technical task, and of necessity the legislator must rely upon the help and advice of recognized experts. In many instances the experts and the lobbyists are one and the same. Yet, in acting in this advisory capacity, these men can serve the public interest at the same time they are serving their own groups.

. . . However, it is equally clear that lobbying does create evils which must be faced if we are to prevent the democratic processes from being perverted. Lobbying is an *evil* when it attempts, through pressures and subterfuges, to obtain approval of special interest legislation that will work against the public welfare. It is with this evil that we should concern ourselves.

. . . To me, the most alarming factor is the tendency of the individual to identify himself so strongly with one of the special interest groups that he neglects the general obligations of citizenship. Inevitably, he will tend to place the demands of his group above that of the national welfare. The "rights" of his particular group become paramount.

. . . One tragic result of the competition between organized blocs for special consideration is that millions of people are being left behind in the economic race. Among the forgotten men of the age are small businessmen, small farmers (four million of them), farm workers, white collar groups, and many professional people. They are not sharing proportionately in the nation's total welfare; they have no vocal, organized groups to plead for their "rights."

Both major parties have naturally responded to the demands of special groups. The tendency has been to meet criticism of favors granted one group by extending similar advantages to other groups. And too many times the decision is based not upon what is right but what is expedient.

. . . More votes are garnered by pointing with pride to specific favors than by oratorical expressions as to the general welfare. However, if we are to meet the challenge which our democracy faces today, more than the idea of winning elections must be considered. The growing strains upon the economic system must be eased, and group demands conflicting with the general welfare must be resisted. Equal justice under law requires constant and disciplined attention.

❖

Faith Steadies the Politician

It is difficult for a politician to speak naturally and without embarrassment of his faith. Some members of our profession have exploited religion, and the understandable reac-

NOTE: *Christian Century,* June 11, 1952.

tion to this offense is to view with suspicion references by individual politicians to religious experience and conviction. I wish we might recapture the atmosphere, once prevailing in America, in which responsible officials could discuss religion without inhibitions.

Early in my own career I determined that I would not identify my candidacy with "a righteous cause." This is not to say that from the standpoint of moral values, political campaigns do not present clear choices. In many races "the right" is distinguishable as favoring one side over the other. I am pointing out, however, that invoking divine approbation for the purpose of gaining favor at the polls is not in our tradition and should be repudiated, as I believe it generally will be. (I recall seeing in a political advertisement in the campaign of 1950 the words "Vote Christian" above a candidate's name. He was overwhelmingly defeated.)

While I believe strongly in the practice of prayer in political matters, I question the use of prayer to seek victory for oneself or a favorite. I prefer the example of one of the country's great pugilists who was once asked if he prayed for victory in the ring. He replied, "Would that be fair? With God on my side the other fellow really wouldn't have much chance; would he?"

It is in the individual determination of grave policy decisions and political judgments that religious guidance has chief significance. My political course has been full of frustration, yet I believe that God has made his strength and his counsel available in the major decisions. I have not sought to determine through prayer a course of expediency and success but rather to find in resort to spiritual resources the answer to the question that stirs the heart of more public men perhaps than the people know, namely, "What is right?"

. . . Even we hardened political workers are entitled to an

occasional retreat to the household of faith. When I am privileged to be out of range of political shafts in the cloisters of faith, I have an opportunity in fellowship and in prayer to gain strength for the dilemmas that politics inevitably provides.

It is with the hope that these personal meditations in a sensitive area of my life will help to convince readers that politics should not be religion's neglected field, that I attempt to express them. From the standpoint of statesmanship the idea was effectively stated by George Washington in his farewell address, in pleading for public morality which he knew could not be maintained without the inspiration of religion. Every useful political career brings one at some stage to an appreciation of the sentiment expressed by Paul, and in such a situation we should be permitted to paraphrase his words, "Neither count I my political life dear unto myself."

The most meaningful experience of my professional life followed one of my early political campaigns in a succession of defeats. Before I was thirty-two years old I had twice been defeated for governor of my state, but in a special election for a congressional seat three years after the second attempt for the governorship, I tried to retrieve something from the efforts I had expended in the intensive campaigns. It was a crucial race for me. I had angered the political leaders of one county in the district and they found an opportunity to punish me. With a registration of only 1,632 they reported 1,850 votes for my opponent, who was the beneficiary rather than the perpetrator of the scheme, and 616 votes for me.

A fraud had obviously been practiced. (Outside of that county I had a lead of 595 votes.) It became the subject of a long and tedious lawsuit. Technicalities blocked my efforts for a recount at every stage, and when at last the judge, a sincere, honest man who wanted to correct a wrong that showed on its face, had to dismiss my case because of higher court rulings, I struggled against human reactions that would impair my faith. But my faith in God and in my fellow man survived that bitter experience. Indeed it was that faith that pulled me through.

. . . I prayed. It might be more accurate to say I talked with God. I asked him not to desert me. I felt that he was on my side.

Here was suffering which was doubly bitter because it was unjust. But I did not want to be embittered or to develop cynicism toward the political system or the people embraced by it. I knew the truth in Henry L. Stimson's words, "Cynicism is the only deadly sin." I asked God to save me from it. I felt at the moment that he was answering my prayer. His presence was as real to me as the judge. The assurance I had as my case was dismissed, that nothing could hurt me if I was not hurt inside, was complete, and I walked out of the room as calm and unperturbed as I have ever been in my life. I hope I can be as sure in future crises that God hears us and provides the strength we need to carry on.

. . . There have been other situations in which I felt the need of falling back upon the resources of faith. One of them came soon after I was elected to Congress, ten years after the experience I have just related. It involved legislation of a highly controversial character and there was considerable feeling about it in my district. I listened attentively to the debate because I was anxious to cast the right vote. I was convinced finally that I should vote against the pending bill. Several of my closest friends used phone calls to urge me to support it. One of them who had been prominent in my campaign was a friend to whom I felt such a strong obligation that it caused me real pain to have to say "no" to him. It was a matter about which he held a strong conviction and I knew what it might mean the severance of our political ties, though not of our friendship. His protests made me realize that I might have to pay with defeat for my own convictions. But I recalled that many others in places of governmental responsibility had faced even greater tests and had subordinated personal interests. Their examples encouraged me.

. . . In the situation confronting me in this early congressional experience it was extremely difficult for me to vote against what I knew to be the prevailing opinion in my district. I wanted to remain in Congress, so the pressures were both political and personal. Most of my closest friends—those who had taken greatest interest in my campaign—were for an "Aye" vote. I was unconvinced by the arguments, and voted "No." Again I had help in prayer. Sitting by an old friend in the House Chamber who remained silent as the roll was called, perhaps because he knew of the conflicts troubling me, I asked God to help me—to give me the inner peace that comes from doing what one knows he should do. Millions had done it before and would do it again. As in the election crisis, I received the assurance that an answered prayer provides. I walked from the Capitol with the same calmness and peace that had come in the earlier experience. From these two experiences I have had my most convincing proof that the eternal God is indeed our certain refuge, and underneath us are the everlasting arms.

Intergovernmental Relations

I have two thoughts in mind about the present situation which finds us philosophically divided in the nation as a whole—states righters on the one hand and centralists or federalists, on the other. This is an oversimplification, I concede. This philosophical division calls for continuing and intelligent study of the role of government in human affairs. I feel that while the emphasis on craftsmanship, the study of legislative methods by which progress can be made without doing violence to our dual form of government, that while legislative skill is extremely important, nevertheless, public understanding also calls for this educational service on our part.

For while we are not editors and are supposed to be servants and not masters of the people, in the field of education we have a great responsibility to stimulate the people to study the problem.

I would suggest for the committee's consideration, for example, that something like the Kestnbaum Commission be established again, next time including participants from the legislatures of our states. We could use this procedure as a means of building into the thinking of members of the general assemblies of the states the importance of this whole system of interrelationships. They still tend to think in legalistic terms since they have not been exposed as fully as we have to the problems through such devices as the Kestnbaum Commission on Inter-Governmental Relations. They see this as a struggle between the states on the one hand and the Federal Government on the other. This sort of struggle for domina-

NOTE: Statement before a subcommittee of the House Government Operations Committee in hearings on intergovernmental relations.

tion does not serve the good of the nation. Whatever our philosophical preferences now in this broad cleavage, it seems to me we ought to accept the preachment of James Madison at the time the Constitution was devised and this unique dual plan of government embraced, that each side must practice reciprocal forbearance. I do not think we can find any better summary of the attitude needed on the part of the respective participants in this struggle and in all power struggles in a moral society, since it seems to me that has to be the spirit of the approach. But we are not yet getting such a spirit.

. . . As a second thing, in an effort to be practical, I would suggest that the committee continue what it is doing, that is to channel to the committees having jurisdiction over specific problems dealt with by the Kestnbaum Commission, after the sifting you can give and the professional aids and interpretations you can supply, all of that body of information compiled during our study. They need it.

They are not always aware of its existence. I find every now and then total unawareness on the part of a legislative committee of some elaborate research that we conducted. It would be very helpful to bridge this gap, and perhaps that is one of the functions of this extremely important committee. You would become in that event not only a monitoring committee but a sort of traffic committee. I point that out as something from which we can all profit.

One interesting thing to me about this whole discussion, this ferment which is very wholesome from my point of view, is that it touches almost every area of governmental activity. There is hardly a problem that is not dealt with in this report. For example, you would think ordinarily that the work of the Foreign Affairs Committee would be only indirectly related to it; yet in a way the problem that committee deals with of preventing war, the problem of war and peace, is so directly related that in a certain sense the most severe aspects of this federal-state relationship grow out of our failure to solve that problem, for the cost of war has necessitated our enlargement of Federal fiscal powers. You can take even these grants-in-aid that go to the states to stimulate some activity. It was often because of the nation's need for security that the stimulation arose and, of course, that is the origin of all grants-in-aid programs, to stimulate activity by the states to provide something that the nation needs.

If you view it historically I think you will find that Federal assistance has been provided either to stimulate, to support, if it is a primary Federal function, or to equalize. And obviously many of these programs grew out of the great disparity in income of the different states of the nation. We can go back to Abraham Lincoln and even well beyond his day to find the origins of Federal aid to schools to overcome this disparity. Certainly we had grant programs in the field of higher education a long time ago, and we should not attach too much importance, it seems to me, to the distinction between higher education and elementary education. Because from the nation's standpoint our stake in education is as profound in elementary education as in higher education.

. . . If you want to stick strictly to the physical side as distinguished from the human side, however, it is easier to get the projection of a Federal program accepted because people do not fear so much the "remote control," the Washington control, where it deals with the physical process. The problem is more difficult on the human side with all the emotional content of a problem of human relations, such as in the field of education in the programs where there is an injection of Federal funds.

Even on the physical side, as late as 1928, we were refusing to project Federal aid into our conservation programs. I am thinking of flood control primarily. I remember how fervently those of us who were victims of the descending floods in the Arkansas Valley had to press upon Congress the need of the people of Arkansas for relief from the flood-waters that fell in Colorado, Kansas, and Oklahoma and yet did their devastation upon Arkansas.

We said there was not any power in Arkansas to meet the problem at Fort Smith by any licensing procedure or anything like that. We can do that with certain types of commerce, have a license issued by our state highway department, which grants the right to use our highways, but the right to use our rivers defied that kind of a police power. So the waters came, and no one questions any more the assertion of a Federal interest in that situation. Neither does anyone as far as I know question the power of the Federal Government to interest itself in the neglect of a hillside farm, though it be a forty-acre farm held by an individual in fee simple in the Arkansas Ozarks.

No one questions on philosophical grounds the right of the Federal Government to say to the owner of that farm: "If in uniting with your neighbors, you can do something to conserve this terrain, the taxpayers of New York will help you do that." That is an obvious national interest. We need to be reminded of these things so we can tell our people that the national interest, even if not paramount, must be recognized as a participating interest. And history is replete with the tragic results of failure to do that.

The city of Antioch came into discussions recently over in the eastern end of the Mediterranean. One time it was a city almost as large as Memphis. Today it is a city of 3,000 people. The beautiful buildings of Antioch are under the silt of the highland that flowed down the rivers of Asia Minor and buried it. There was no central authority that interested itself in a city with a source of wealth that supported a population of 300,000 people, and so its fate was sealed.

. . . Even in this good old American tradition of democracy in which people advance alternative solutions, it seems to me that there must be a flexibility of thought. I see no hope for us if we are to struggle against change. With regard to this matter of mobility—both of wealth and of people because they seem to go together—you have a fugacious character of wealth and a migrant aspect of human life, of society, both of which are in the background of all of these questions having to do with intergovernmental relations. One thing that has troubled me is how to find out what it is that explains our differences. It isn't that we who stand for Federal aid, for example, pursuing that illustration, love the children any more than the others; I would freely concede that, as one of the speakers the other day asked us to concede. I know this isn't true. I think, however, that the real difference is that we have not yet conditioned ourselves to the necessity of making our Government resilient and I believe that the Founding Fathers intended it to be resilient.

They came up with the answer, you will remember, which was the Virginia plan that roughly gave us the present charter for power, the division and the delineation of power. The National Government—and I am speaking now not of the United States as a Federal Government, we have overdone that, we are not a government of just delegated powers, we are a sovereign government with residual powers reserved to the states—we, the people, fashioned a national government, given certain powers, based on the faith that it would not be overdone or usurped or projected unduly into intimate affairs. This organization was based on the concept of the Federal Government's doing two things, first, what the states could not or would not do for themselves, and second, what if done by the states would be done with damage to their neighbors.

That was the simple formula by which they fashioned the Constitution. That leaves a lot of room for new assertion of power. It raises this question though for our times: Does it really relieve the men in the local governments of the responsibility they must have or must retain and must exercise if we make progress at the national level and if the democratic concept is preserved? I pointed this issue out to one of the governors who fought pretty vigorously against some of the things I said to the committee today. One of the governors said, "You are far away from us and local government. Being far away from us in geographical terms is not good for the people." That is a postulate, I know, that is often asserted. Yet I challenge it.

Sometimes there is less efficiency where the decision is made in proximity and greater efficiency where it is further removed. The political pressures in the immediate vicinity are often overpowering.

. . . It isn't necessarily true that the folks close to a problem can provide the most efficient decisions. When I pursued this issue with the governor on the Kestnbaum Commission, I said, "I venture I saw Jim Ferguson living in Perry County, Arkansas, more often in the last ten years than the governor of Arkansas, who lives only fifty miles from him." Why does he see me more often? I am one of six. The governor is the equivalent of six of us. I had an area only a hundred miles long and I could get over to Perry County more often than the governor could. When Jim Ferguson was talking to me, he was channeling information to his Federal Government. That is a truism of course that no one would challenge. I was talking to Jim Ferguson over the radio every Sunday and he was getting a weekly letter from me. The fact that I was a thousand miles from him doesn't alter the basic relationship. The Federal Government was pretty close to him. I don't think we ought to be quite as apologetic as we are sometimes about the remoteness of Washington control. There ought to be less emotionalism about the decisions that are made in Washington as we visualize the impact made on the Jim Fergusons in the little villages.

. . . The neglect of rural life is a challenge to those of us who represent rural areas because certainly the sociological side of the problem has been neglected.

The rural constituents have no right to disregard the new concentrations of population in the cities, but on the other hand the masses of the cities must remember that there are reserved rural resources that are vital to their welfare. I should like again to put in larger perspective this question of change in making decisions so that we can secure as much resilience as possible.

I think the cities have suffered a good deal by reason of this rural domination. They have been regarded as the wards of the states by the Federal Government, and then they have been victimized by this condition of rural voting strength in state legislatures to which Mr. Kestnbaum pointed this morning. So they have suffered. That is the reason some of the mayors told us that when problems like getting better airports came up, they looked to Washington and not to the state capitals. We have to find some practical answers. I do not like ever to see the Federal Government bypassing the states. I think there is a great danger there, and we would help more in the prescribing of general criteria that force the states to be fair to the cities than to push the states out of the way and go direct to the cities except in a very limited number of legislative situations. I think on the question of financial help, however, that we would not impair this principle of which I speak if we could set up—and do it pretty quickly—a plan of payments in lieu of taxes to the cities where we are taking over commercial and industrial property and denying them a source of revenue. . . .

III Civil Rights in a Southern Context

Persistently, since in the 1930's he first advocated repeal of the poll tax as a prerequisite to voting, Brooks Hays has sought for means of improving relationships between the races, finding common ground between the Northern and Southern wings of the Democratic party and introducing a basis of local consent into the application of the Supreme Court decision in the school cases.

❖

Lanham of Georgia on the Hays Proposals

Mr. LANHAM. Mr. Speaker, we have been commemorating the birthday of one of America's true noblemen, Abraham Lincoln. I am glad that we of the South can join with those of you from the North in paying tribute to this great American. We now see that had he lived, many of the unspeakable indignities we had to suffer would not have been our lot.

At one time when some of the more violent men of ill will were urging harsher treatment for the South, Mr. Lincoln replied that he had not suffered at the hands of the South but with the South. Were he alive today, I am sure that again he would suffer with the South at the threat of the enactment of force laws that would inevitably bring another tragic era for our beloved Southland.

NOTE: *Congressional Record*, February 14, 1949; a speech in the House of Representatives by the Honorable Henderson Lanham of Georgia.

88

A few days ago the gentleman from Arkansas, the Honorable Brooks Hays, spoke from the well of this House words of such reasonableness and sanity that I wish every one of you would study and heed them. I am not prepared to say that I would agree in every detail with the proposed plan for the settlement of the so-called civil rights question. But I do commend to you the spirit of good will and understanding that pervades Mr. Hays's proposals. It is from this approach that a fair and equitable settlement of the issues involved can be evolved.

A few days ago I heard a friend gently chide the gentleman from Arkansas (Mr. Hays) with the charge that he was "always floating around on a cloud." He admitted that occasionally the gentleman from Arkansas (Mr. Hays) parked his cloud and came down to earth. In this age of materialism and cynicism I am sure we need more cloud floaters. For "where there is no vision the people perish.". . . His head may be in the clouds where the winds of God's truth can reach him, but his feet are firmly planted upon the ground. His is that rare combination of vision and practicality.

. . . I call upon the Members on each side of the aisle to study his proposals and to approach the problem with the same degree of sanity and reasonableness that characterizes Mr. Hays's thinking on the subject.

With the Speaker's leave, I include with my remarks an editorial from the *Atlanta Constitution* commenting on the Hays plan, and an article by Gladstone Williams that appeared in the same newspaper:

Southerners are planning to introduce in Congress this week their own version of a civil rights program.

It is being introduced by men of good will and good intent. The plan is to get it before the Congress ahead of any administration bills.

We urge thoughtful southerners to have a look at it. In brief it would do these three things:

1. It would provide for a constitutional amendment to abolish the poll tax. Since 41 states, including Georgia, have already abolished it and others are preparing to do so, there is no doubt but that the poll tax will go and that it would do so without any Federal coercion.

2. Lynching would come under Federal statute. This newspaper has always opposed Federal coercion, and still does. But there can no longer be any doubt but that failure of local peace officers to enforce laws against such violence properly has created so much national anger and opinion that it is not longer possible to avoid some such measure.

. . . The honest southerner must admit that local law-enforcement agencies, because of the peculiarities of our political methods, frequently are powerless to proceed against a prominent family or one politically powerful when such is involved in a lynching case. This is wrong, but it is a fact. The southerners propose to remove a lynching case from the county where it occurs and try it in a county where the local passions and political blocs would not apply.

3. The southerners plan to introduce legislation which would establish in the Department of Labor a board which would have the power to investigate, conciliate, arbitrate, and recommend in cases involving discrimination in employment. This avoids the Federal police feature, and it bypasses the unconstitutional proposal that a man may be told he must hire someone whether that person is acceptable or not. It was exactly this system which worked so well during the recent World War in cases involving thousands of workers from minority groups. There is no reason to think it will not work even better now when the national conscience is so much more aware of the evils and wrongs of discrimination. A standing army could not enforce the provisions of the FEPC as proposed by the more radical makers of civil rights legislation.

We recommend this plan to thoughtful southerners as reasonable and as being possible of excellent results. . . .

(From the *Atlanta Constitution* of February 7, 1949)
HAYS RIGHTS PLAN A TEST OF GOOD FAITH
(By Gladstone Williams)

Washington.—In an effort to remove civil rights legislation from the field of bitter controversy, Representative Brooks Hays, Democrat, of Arkansas, has come forward with a well-reasoned compromise program that should appeal to moderates on both sides of the question. Without a compromise there is danger of Congress being split wide open on the issue. The Senate Rules Committee is now wrestling with the problem of strengthening cloture rules in order to give President Truman's civil rights program a fair chance of passage. Southern Senators are determined to wage a last-ditch fight against any change in the rules which would deny them the right to unlimited debate in discussing controversial legislation of the kind.

. . . Mr. Hays, a southerner himself, calls for concessions from extremists on both sides of the racial question. If the moderates on both sides will approach the problem in the spirit of compromise, he believes it will be possible to work out a civil rights program that will be acceptable to all concerned and generally meet the objectives sought by the President.

. . . The compromise Representative Hays proposes calls for this:

First, he would limit Federal anti-segregation policies to movements in interstate transportation–travel.

Second, he would repeal poll-tax requirements for voting by constitutional amendment, rather than by statute.

Third, he would have enacted a modified antilynching law which would leave primary responsibility for dealing with mob violence to the individual states and local communities, with the Federal Government empowered to step in only when the state and local authorities failed to act.

Fourth, he would abandon all proposals for a Federal law for coercion in employment, and instead would set up a counseling service in the Department of Labor to work for nondiscrimination in industry.

As the Arkansas man points out, there seems no need for further legislation to achieve the President's objective of nonsegregation in interstate travel because of the Supreme Court decision invalidating a Virginia statute requiring the segregation of white and Negro passengers in interstate travel.

. . . So far as the poll tax goes, Mr. Hays is entirely willing to have Congress submit the question to the various states in the form of a constitutional amendment . . .

On antilynching measures, he reminds that that is an evil that has practically been extinguished, so that it is no longer the issue it once was. He sees no reason why a compromise should not be reached whereby the Federal Government would step in only after local authorities had failed to do something, and with the penalties and fines now proposed being eliminated.

The Hays program is certainly worthy of careful consideration by all those who honestly would like to see some effective civil rights legislation enacted. It opens the way for a meeting of minds among the moderates, though the extremists may be expected to raise their voices in opposition on both sides.

It will probably offer the test of whether the extremists are really interested in seeing a constructive program adopted, or whether they merely prefer to keep the issue alive for its political effect.

❖

The Little Rock Situation

M r. President and fellow Lions, there have been occasions during my service in Congress when I have wished that I might get all of my constituents together for a heart-to-heart talk. This is such an occasion. The time has come for me to open my mind to the people of this city which has honored me and to review my role in the discussions and events leading to the President's action in installing troops at our high school.

I speak to you out of a heavy heart. If it is an imposition,

NOTE: A speech to the Little Rock Lions Club, September 25, 1957, two days after riots at Little Rock Central High School and one day after the arrival of troops to enforce integration.

I ask your forgiveness. But what better forum could I find than that of this civic club, of which I have been a member thirty-two years, devoted as it is to high ideals and free from partisanship and sectarianism. There was wisdom in what a British statesman said who, confronted by the chairman at a speaking engagement, was told that he could speak upon any subject he liked except religion and politics. Said he, "Finding that I could not speak upon the two subjects of greatest importance to mankind, I promptly left." Now I am familiar with the Lions' code. I know that politics and religion are not banned, only their partisan and sectarian aspects.

As a public official, the only one elected by the people of this area for a national responsibility, I have tried to be helpful in providing a bridge between the two units of government—state and federal.

. . . My interest has been only secondarily in the political forces. Our first effort must be in the direction of easing tensions and healing wounds caused by the bitter controversy which surrounds us.

I shall say nothing today that I would not want my colored constituents to hear, nor am I trying to talk anyone, segregationist or integrationist, into a different point of view regarding the current debate—for that is not the paramount issue. Neither should the conflicting ideologies in the federal-state relations debate be given much time at this moment. The issue is: Shall lawless elements have their way, or shall our traditional devotion to the orderly processes of law be maintained? On this question we must be united.

We have suffered terribly in recent days. Our pride has been wounded. National publicity has not been favorable. We fear that we have been damaged in the eyes of the nation and the world. It is not too late to retrieve this situation for

I am sure we have not been permanently damaged. It is true that we are the focus of attention in every part of the world—the great drama that has captured the interest of the masses of men everywhere has moved upon the local scene—and what we decide may have tremendous significance in the course of history. This is a fateful period. It is a time for a rededication on our part to the constitutional system under which we live.

My part in this drama was self-imposed. It resulted from my reflections of Sunday afternoon, September 8. On Monday I was convinced that I should at least offer my help, and so I called my long-time, devoted friend, Sherman Adams, with whom I had served in Congress. Our friendship lies completely outside partisan loyalties. I said, "Do you think of anything I might do to help in this situation?" He was interested. He asked me to suggest some steps that might be taken, and I told him I thought it would be helpful if the heads of government, state and federal, might sit down together. He reminded me that I had initiated the idea, that it would not be proper for the White House to assume that the Governor wanted to talk to the President, but that if the Governor would come with a constructive attitude of mind, a discussion of the crisis might be helpful. I asked the Governor for an appointment—and within moments I was at the Mansion talking over the possibilities. His attitude was in conformity with Sherman Adams' statement; so arrangements were made for the trip to Newport. His request for a conference was promptly granted. He asked me to go with him. You are familiar with the story and I shall not dwell upon the details. The President also was co-operative, and it seems to me that in spite of the disappointing events of recent days, some good was accomplished. Conditions would be worse today if the meeting had not taken place.

Now there were no deals. It was recognized at all stages that each executive had firm opinions regarding the responsibility of his office, and we are now in conflict because of the different interpretations given to the task by these heads of government.

My political faith has been nurtured by Southern institutions. I am a product of the South. I know its point of view, and I believe that my legislative record reflects some understanding of its problems, but the time has come for us to appraise new and powerful forces in the world's life, to determine if a more flexible attitude might not be necessary if our dual form of government is to survive. We are indeed "an indestructible union of indestructible States," but an unreasoning resistance to any change whatever might provoke the very actions which we fear.

Year after year I have seen our vote in opposition to unreasonable civil rights laws gradually reduced until today both Houses of Congress perhaps are impotent in the face of demands by the rest of the nation for concessions to change. This does not mean that our non-Southern friends are intolerant or offensive. To be sure, there are extremists among them who would humiliate us. But until this year we have convinced our colleagues that Federal action of any kind would be unfair, and even under terrific pressures the congressional majority in the current session made important concessions to the Southern viewpoint in producing the first civil rights law since Reconstruction. In a sense it was a victory for the Southern moderates, but if we do not act with supreme wisdom in the months ahead, we will disarm those who stand between us and the political interests which would move speedily in the South through Federal legislation and conceivably further Federal military action. The tragic results can be easily predicted. Time is an essential element in this whole operation. I insist that not many want to humiliate the South. The problem is not a result of a "hate-the-South" movement, though I am pained that some outside the region are blind to the complexities of our problem.

There are many reasons why we must be calm and temperate in our judgments. The demand for change cannot be dismissed with the claim that agitators and outsiders are responsible for our troubles. I believe that the colored citizen is apt to live a happier life in Little Rock than in Chicago, for example, though I must speak with restraint here since this could easily be attributed to provincialism. I am confident that the distress of our city is but one symptom of a malaise that troubles the nation and the world. This could happen anywhere and considering our good record it is something that should not have happened to our city. We deserve better than this. As we weigh the differences between Chicago and Little Rock, whatever the irritations there—and they are great, for the problem of the colored man in the North has assumed large proportions—it must be conceded that in Chicago he has been relieved of the official stigma which remains where segregation is imposed by force of law.

I know that spokesmen for the Negro, the wisest and best among them, mean what they say when they indicate that they do not believe that progress for their people lies in the proposal to throw together in every classroom white and colored pupils just for the sake of putting them in proximity to each other as they study. This would be not only a meaningless innovation, but poor educational policy. If New York City cares to try it out—as apparently they wish to do—the experiment will doubtless have little value for us. Trusted Negro leaders do however expect us to take their viewpoint and their aspirations into account. They prefer that we stop doing things for them and begin doing things with them.

I shall not dwell upon the aspirations of the colored people. Certainly we cannot expect them to withhold demands that their constitutional rights be accorded them, or that they not be given the benefits of new laws designed to help them, even though the law might be exceedingly unpopular with their white friends and neighbors. The enforcement of law is not limited to popular laws. Constitutional forms are maintained only when people are completely dedicated to the ideal of law and order without reference to its impingement upon some cherished practices of their own.

There must be, it seems to me, a greater flexibility in our own thinking as we proceed to adapt ourselves to conditions produced by the recent startling decisions of the high court. I might point out that the troubles we now experience were predicted by some of us who knew what the impact of forced desegregation would be. The *Saturday Evening Post* of November 8, 1952, recorded my words warning against the "sudden liquidation of segregation." I do not gloat over that prediction's being proved correct. I fervently wish it might have been proved wrong.

Now surely there are lessons in the Little Rock experience for both sides. For the South the lesson is that in any community where the execution of Federal court orders approving locally determined integration plans are interfered with by any threat of violence, and the local and state enforcement agencies for any reason are inadequate, leaving the community exposed to the fury of a mob, Federal enforcement may be carried out even by military operations. It should be noted, however, that the use of Federal troops in Little Rock cannot be said to have set a definite precedent for the use of force in determining the degree or character of school integration in a given community.

For the non-South there is also something to ponder in the

Little Rock story. Surely the nation in applauding the 1954 decisions in their long-range application will recognize that military enforcement of the nation's will is not an acceptable policy. There are urgent reasons for the rest of the country's recognizing the validity of our plea for time. Great damage to national unity will result if this lesson goes unheeded.

Let me speak briefly of the moral and spiritual phases of this problem. Some of the most heartwarming letters I received upon my election as president of the Southern Baptist Convention were from men of other faiths. I recall, for example, the letter from Msgr. Ligutti, adviser to the Pope on rural problems. My Catholic friend pointed out that in attacking economic problems doctrinal differences are not important. Letters from Jewish friends have been equally inspiring and served to remind me that the social values for which we are guardians are a common heritage.

Every segment of our population is affected by the threat of lawlessness such as we witnessed on Monday. Ask the supervisors of the parochial school not far from Central High School how they felt when vagrants wandered into their neighborhood to throw rocks in the direction of church property. Here was a menacing force that unrestrained would destroy our religious as well as civic liberties.

I have been asked by many people, "Should Billy Graham come to Little Rock?" The answer is, "Yes, but not now." The patient is in a state of shock, and I am sure the doctor would say, "The chaplain's visit would help, but ask him not to come until religious counsel and consolation can be appreciated." Moreover, a visit by this famous and talented preacher, my good friends, would, if ill-timed, hurt our pride by the implication that we must be singled out for moral judgments. There are aspects of our community life that require and justify evangelism of a high order, but the symptoms of our illness are found in many places across the land and around the world. If our pride should be damaged too sorely, preachments would be of no avail.

Still, I am eager to see Billy Graham. Perhaps he can speak effectively to the two groups who need to be confronted. One, those who caused so much trouble by overt acts. For them repentance might be difficult. The other group perhaps embraces all of us, at least to some extent. Indifference and materialism have taken a toll. We have failed to deal adequately with the causes of the trouble. There are constant appeals to church people for sympathy and for understanding of the minority aspirations. I have always felt that within the framework of our own Southern life probably there is a capacity for progress in this field, but it will not be easy, and progress will not be possible until we recapture an atmosphere of good will and mutual respect.

Now there are international phases of this problem and they are very real; they are pronounced. The world is in a crisis and our enemy is powerful. He will exploit our failures and we cannot afford to give him any advantage. Do not misunderstand me. I am not suggesting that we must base our action upon eagerness to surpass the Communists' global strategy. Surely there is a nobler incentive. In this field we must do what is right because it is *right*. I recognize that even a perfect performance is not likely to induce the Soviets to change their propaganda methods. They will continue to lie about us.

We can take the President at his word that the Federal troops now in Little Rock, whose very presence postpones essential steps toward a solution, will be withdrawn when conditions he described in his radio talk are met. I am sure that whatever differences we have as to the constitutionality of his actions or the propriety of his decisions, they must have been painful to him. He is eager for us to have the responsibility locally for law enforcement and to have adequate facilities for putting down lawlessness. Local enforcement powers must be utilized. Latent leadership must be stirred to action. Our police force which performed well on Monday must have our full support.

Again, let me emphasize that the issue is not integration or Federal authority in school matters, but rather how to deal with lawlessness. Segregationists and integrationists, Republicans and Democrats can unite in this cause.

IV *International Co-operation and World Peace*

Member since 1951 of the powerful Committee on Foreign Affairs, Brooks Hays has had a part in processing the legislation brought before the House of Representatives in one of the fields of his greatest interest.

❖

The Continuing Quest for World Peace

Every representative must undertake constantly to balance those interests that are local and regional in character, and those that have a national import. And in these times as America proceeds into a crucial period of transition, accepting rather reluctantly her position as the free world's leader, there is, of course, the obligation upon all of us to think of America's greatness in terms of the welfare of other peoples, and not in terms of our own narrow national interests.

And so it is with a broad concept of true internationalism, in its soundest sense, that I speak of our concern in the Congress today for peace. I know sometimes peace lovers are inclined to give up the struggle; the peace seems so tenuous and insecure. It is like an illness. The patient is very sick, and because he fears an operation is necessary he says to the doctor, "Let's have it over with—let's get it back of us."

NOTE: Address at the installation banquet of the 31st Annual Convention of Civitan International, Jacksonville, Florida, June, 1951.

So it is with fear. Some of our people, fearing that the war is inevitable, say to the Congress, "Let's use our strength while we have an advantage; let's inaugurate the war ourselves."

But it is my feeling that however great the odds may be against us, stated mathematically, we must continue to struggle for peace. Peace on honorable terms, but with the feeling that an honorable peace is still possible, that America must not renounce her historic ideals and launch what is called a preventive war.

. . . We of the Congress enter into the experiences of our people more perhaps than is known. When I read the statistics of the casualties in Korea, I see them not as figures but as homes that have contributed loved ones in a faraway place to preserve our freedom.

I think that was in the mind of Lincoln when he spoke of the "mystic chords of memory stretching from every battle-field and every patriot grave to every living heart and hearth-stone." We do share the heartaches and aspirations of our people.

Now let me speak of the negative side of this quest for peace, first the things that we must avoid if we make the peace that is so tenuous now, firm and secure for the future.

It is doubtless apparent from what I have said that I believe we must not retreat. Now we have come to the position of world leadership reluctantly. The nation is not spiritually conditioned for it yet, for two oceans separate us from the quarrels of the other world, in the Pacific and the Atlantic, and we still wonder why we are inevitably drawn into their conflicts. Our cultures are so different and so many of our purposes seem to conflict. Still we cannot escape them. Our advocacy of participation in world affairs is not born of a wish to serve other nations at the expense of our own, but a recognition that we are inextricably bound up with their destiny.

We must not retreat, whatever the temptation, whatever the cost. We must accept as a physical fact our proximity to aggression and our identification with intended victims closest to it. Almost every member of Congress, whatever his political preferences, recognizes this inexorable condition.

Secondly, we must not appease. I shall not labor the point because I am sure this audience would share my convictions that the men who preside over the Soviet system are cruel and tyrannical, that their ambitions are serious, and that they are intent upon a military conquest of the world, if it is possible.

. . . Finally, we must not undertake to dominate the world. Now we have the power, of course, to do great things for all the nations of the world, and sometimes when the requirements seem to overwhelm us, we must remember that our capacity industrially is stupendous.

Paul Hoffman gave us this charting of progress recently— just fifty years ago America had 6 per cent of the world's population and was producing 20 per cent of its wealth. Today, with 7 per cent, just a little more of its population, we are producing not 20 per cent, but 50 per cent of its goods; and so by reason of our tremendous material and physical strength we are pre-eminently the world's leader.

The important thing, however, is that we match these enormous powers industrially with a moral and intellectual leadership that is commensurate. And I know that your fellow Civitans at home will respond to the summons to a world task, for it is a challenge to the wonderful ideals that find expression in your creed.

. . . I must return to my point that American domination must be avoided. Among the political leaders of the country are some who are *not* sure about this third point. They believe that the United States, having expended so much money for the rehabilitation of the world, may properly claim the right to make decisions for the world. As I see it, that leads to another fallacy, the replacement of a dying geographical isolationism, by spiritual and moral isolationism.

It would be fatal to this country if we should undertake to withdraw ourselves from world conferences, if we should make our decisions without reference to the interests and the needs and the desires of other nations.

Now the full implications must be pondered, for we have our obligations to the American taxpayer, and he is a harried individual. The Congress is placing new burdens on him, but you can be sure that the action pains every sensitive person in the Congress.

It is only because we are convinced that the dangers are great and that the fear of war is real, not artificial, that we make these preparations for it. Yet if we should do nothing else, we would betray our trust, we would be faithless to you. Building up tremendous armaments in the hope that military might will save us is only a part of our duty.

. . . I have spoken of the three things we must not do. We must not retreat, we must not appease, we must not dominate. Now let me speak of the positive aspects of our evolving foreign policy.

First, I am confident that you will agree with this: We must make this a bipartisan effort in the truest and finest sense. My party has been honored with leadership for a long time.

. . . And yet I am convinced that without the resources of the opposition party, we of the Congress cannot do our work acceptably. In other words, the task is so great that nothing less than the total resources of both the Republican and the Democratic parties, the intellectual and moral resources of these two great parties, will suffice.

. . . Secondly, we must find practical ways of improving the United Nations. I hope very much that you will agree with me, for this is a period in which we must have not only the kind of unity between the parties at home to which I have just alluded, but that degree of co-operation that binds the free nations together with striking power if war comes, to build first the deterrent force to avoid war if possible, but to win if hopes of peace are frustrated.

It is one of the hazards of democratic life that we must achieve by democratic means the unity that the Soviets acquire by tyrannical means. We must settle our differences right out in the open.

. . . The year 1950 was significant because for the first time in history the United States with other nations fought under the mandate of the United Nations to prevent aggression. That decision, I believe, will be referred to a thousand years from now as an historic decision and one of the turning points in man's long struggle for peace and stability.

. . . I like one thing about your creed. You refer to the human mind and its commitments to the rule of law. This "rule of law" is a phrase with tremendous meaning. The whole concept of a United Nations is to elevate to the world level that which we have become so accustomed to in America that we are scarcely aware of it, the settlement of conflicts by judicial principle.

This whole venture in international order is very simple. It is the effort to achieve the rule of law, to apply judicial principles to conflicts between nations. That calls for a lot of practical work, good craftsmanship by Congress, by our representatives in the United Nations.

The world court must acquire a wider jurisdiction, more carefully defined, and something must be done about the veto privilege which has been abused so often by Russia.

Finally, we must put into our world leadership a greater moral concept. The nineteenth century was Britain's, but the twentieth century can be ours. As one of my friends said, "I am sure it will either be ours or Russia's." If we claim it, it must be said, too, that it was humanity's century. Just as Great Britain, supplying the leadership that seemed essential to holding the world together, gave it the impress of commerce, so America in the twentieth century must give it the impress of moral power. I am sure of that.

I believe that out of new devotions to these common ends —the attainment of justice and liberty, the achievement of the rule of law in our world—there will be the grandest demonstration of faith that a people ever had.

Therefore, may I close by referring to the origin of my own faith. I want to refer to my father, a wise and good man, a country lawyer who gave me something that has helped me through many a difficult struggle. My father taught me that there is something in my equipment as a lawyer that was not of my making. The love of justice, he said, is native. The law school could provide a certain art in giving it expression and help me to embellish its administration, but the love of justice which inhabits the heart of a man, he insisted, is there because the loving God above has planted it within me.

I am indebted to my father for that delicate delineation of a beautiful thought. I pass it on to you here. I am not invading the realm of the theologian; you see, I am speaking still as a lawyer, but my father was right. Isn't it logical, then, to assume that it is universal? If the Eternal put it in my heart to seek justice and liberty, a young lawyer in the foothills of the Ozarks, untrained, undistinguished, isn't it logical to assume that God has planted it in the hearts of people across the oceans, in the hearts of the Russians, the Chinese?

This is the only basis for a hope that there can be a world united—if not in our time, in some future period. I believe it is true that the same love of freedom and the same love of justice—strange impulses to the rulers of the Kremlin—at least exist in the hearts of their subject people, and our quarrel is not with the masses of their enslaved nations. They are victims of a tyranny that has overtaken many peoples of the past, a form of slavery we do not propose to have overrun the Western world, but we recognize its victims as our fellow creatures. . . .

I come to this final conclusion, that the hope for peace has a spiritual quality. It is a part of the ideal you Civitans are exalting in cities across the continent. We must not tire of the quest for peace. We will not retreat, we will not appease, we will not dominate. On the other hand, we will struggle for a bipartisan foreign policy, a strengthened United Nations to inspire and help other free peoples acquire strength for the defense of freedom, and finally to give moral content and moral power to a program that convinces the captives that the voice of justice and freedom within them is a more authentic voice than that of Karl Marx's apostles, who talk of materialism and power.

The American ideal is indeed the hope of the world. International aspirations are consistent with the truest nationalism as Americans know it. As Lincoln said, it is here that "we may meanly lose or nobly save the last best hope of earth."

Technical Assistance: Instrument of National Policy

Many of the independent nations of the world cherish their independence, but they do not fully appreciate the nature of the East-West conflict. Most of them, I am sure, would recognize in case of armed aggression that they do have a stake in the issue that divides the communist and the free world.

Without neglecting the importance of a strong military defense, we must share our productiveness with the less favored peoples of the world. Even if we were not thinking in terms of global strategy against communism, we should be busy convincing the "neutral" third of the world's population that we are gravely concerned with assistance programs that are only remotely related to our own narrow national interests. This involves our ideals. It involves the philosophy upon which we have built our nation.

There are political implications in these world programs. The businessman fears that the cost may be too much, although the UN proper, with all its organizational activities, takes only eight cents per year from the U. S. taxpayer, and when we add the activities of the Specialized Agencies, the total cost is still only sixty-seven cents per U. S. citizen per year. Some of our people fear that energies are diverted that could be used at home. It is difficult to establish that in promoting world progress we promote our own self-interest. But it is true, and we must try to be convincing on that point. There are also considerations outside the appeal of our national self-interest. Underneath the surface of mental skepticism is a potential nobility in the heart of the American voter,

NOTE: Address at Conference on University Contracts Abroad, Michigan State University, November 17, 1955.

108

and he has springs of generosity and intelligence that can be channeled in constructive directions.

Some of the most interesting things that were talked over in United Nations meetings this year concerned the UN technical assistance programs. One of the Expanded Technical Assistance Program's functions is to co-ordinate the work of such Specialized Agencies as the World Health Organization, the UN Children's Fund, the Food and Agriculture Organization, and the International Postal Union. These multilateral operations are extremely important for the underdeveloped countries. Multilateral programs spread the burden, and other nations are eager to assume some of the responsibilities for them.

Every person recovering from a dread disease through miracle drugs feels grateful to find that some of them were discovered in foreign laboratories. The farmers who are aware of the benefits of research abroad, and of the help in their fight against crop diseases, feel a new sense of internationalism. The interdependence of our modern world is, of course, something that I do not need to labor. But perhaps we talk too much of what we have done for other people and too little of our debt to them. We should impress our own people with the fact of interdependence, and certainly we should avoid every appearance of trying to impose our own culture on other peoples.

There is an impression among those who have not probed deeply the question of political sentiment that we should retreat from responsibilities for leadership in education and health and material progress throughout the world. While we cannot read the Russians' minds or appraise their decisions, it is evident that they are transferring some of their energies away from the military into the economic and propaganda fields. We must not let them outrun us. We must be in there fighting for the kind of bold, effective technical assistance program that convinces the people of the world that we are concerned about living standards, and that the people of the United States want to share our incredible productivity with them. If we move into blighted areas and neglected places with imagination and leadership, we will win in this global struggle with the communists, and nothing can obstruct us. I fear that if we follow a pinch-penny policy for technical assistance and foreign aid, we may lose this race to those who believe altogether differently about man, about human society, and about the processes of government by which order and justice are sought.

We are making headway. The technical assistance program is being accepted, and I think it is because of the fine admixture of practical values with our historic ideal of service. Every poll I have seen supports this. Only 6 per cent of the college-educated people are opposed; 94 per cent are for it. The percentage in favor goes down a little, according to the polls, if specific sums are mentioned. They always look too big, whatever the figure, but the principle is embedded in the thinking of the American people, and even in the group of the lowest educational level—the grammar school level—50 per cent know about technical assistance and are generally for it.

The technical assistance program should not be greatly affected by changes in the administration or control of Congress. We must have the total resources of both parties to prevail in this great human service. There is too much suffering abroad, and there are too many expectations of us, to leave unutilized our tremendous moral and intellectual resources.

V The Baptist Layman

In college, Brooks Hays's nickname was "deacon." At the age of twenty-four he was made a deacon by the First Baptist Church of Russellville, Arkansas. From then on, in assignments of widening scope culminating in his election as president of the Southern Baptist Convention in 1957, he has viewed his world as a Christian's workshop.

❖

Baptists and World Tasks

Mr. President and brother Baptists: I am grateful for the high privilege of occupying one of the greatest forums of this postwar year, 1947. I am pleased that the sessions are being held in Denmark, which has with its Scandinavian neighbors, contributed so much to the building of America. Many of us know something of the thrilling story of Denmark's agricultural progress. We appreciate particularly its spiritual implications, for, underlying the great land reforms was the concept that "the earth is the Lord's." Nations like individuals must have ideals of stewardship. . . .

A thousand of us have come from America for these sessions. We want to understand you and your problems in Europe and we want to be understood by you. We must have understanding if we make our fight together for a decent world.

Note: Address at the Seventh Congress of the Baptist World Alliance, Copenhagen, Denmark, July, 1947.

A French lady once said to me, "You cannot understand us because you have not suffered." But she was mistaken. We have, and some among us have suffered greatly. It is true also that some have been unaware of the suffering of their neighbors—too concerned with the absorbing interests of prosperous America. On the other hand, millions have endured grief and personal pain in the war and there is a widespread consciousness in American churches of your privations and sacrifices. Great tribulations unite us.

Now we cannot meet the appeal of stricken Europe without using the processes of a Christian government. Our church resources are hopelessly inadequate for such a task. One of the last actions of the American Congress before its recent adjournment was the appropriation of $1,600,000,000 for Europe's aid. It was not a partisan move—it was supported by both political parties. Many of us in the Congress believe that the parties must forget their differences in this monumental effort to save Western civilization. . . .

This past year it has been hard for us at home—eating better than Americans have ever eaten—to grasp the fact of war's ruin, and the malnutrition and discouragement that are its inevitable result. It is only human I suppose at the end of a war to want to push unpleasant facts out of sight.

But if Americans come over here this summer, eat as we have been eating at one of the few tables in Europe where food can be spread in relative plenty, and then go home and say those other facts do not exist, we shall have done a major disservice to our fellow citizens in the Western world whose share of our wartime alliance was so much heavier than our own. And we shall have done a disservice to the Christian community in whose name our voyage was undertaken.

It is obvious from our discussions here that we believe the

world's current crisis is a concern of organized religion. We believe that mankind has a destiny in this world as well as in another. Our beloved Dr. Truett used to say that one reason we know so little about the other world is that it was God's deliberate decision not to detract from the critical importance of this earthly existence.

I speak as an American and as a Baptist layman and—if I may use a word that is flavored with some prejudice—as a politician. Some of my first lessons in the functioning of democratic government were in a Baptist congregation, and my concept of democracy as a community of free men is associated with this experience. The commonwealth is one of the Christian's workshops.

We have experienced in our generation some of history's supreme tragedies in the seizure by perverse and evil men of the processes of state. Many have come, therefore, to look upon the state as essentially evil—but its good or its evil is rather the good and evil in us. Political patterns will always yield to human efforts—when vigorously exerted—to bring them into conformity with Christian principles. I speak primarily of America's responsibility because of our present position of leadership and I want that leadership to have moral power. Whether we have it or not depends upon Christian forces primarily of our country but to some extent of the world.

The governments under which we all live are much involved in the great enterprise of extending liberty and perfecting the processes of law for its security in a peaceful world. The modern Christian state though not the source of liberty is nevertheless its guardian and must be physically and morally strong.

Liberty is the heritage of millions, but for vast populations it remains only a hope and a pursuit. It is too often conceived of as exclusively a political matter. Historically its roots are in religion. It is not the gracious gift of the state but the inherent right of men and women as God's creatures. Our most famous philosopher of the West, Thomas Jefferson, won its acceptance in America's constitutional law on this basis. God willed us to be free—in the highest sense—free to worship or not to worship, to assemble, to utter our grievances, and to be unrestrained by any political power in the exercise of basic human rights. To the sovereignty of the human soul every power of the state must yield. What a world this would be if all of its rulers would accept these simple Christian truths!

. . . No government that cherishes individual freedom has anything to fear from Baptists. Our church bodies have not thrust themselves between the individual and the state. Our spokesmen have protested threatened invasions of our prerogatives, but we have left to the state the adjudication of conflicts and have avoided arbitrary positions as a group. The taxing of our wealth, the policing of our activities, the exercise of the state's prerogative of making secure its citizens in their lives and property will always have our loyal support for the state must reserve its right to the final word in borderland issues. This requires a bold faith on our part. Standing for ecclesiastical decentralization, we have no power to match even the weakest government. Where we have had a chance to try out the idea, however, our faith that popular governments under the nourishment of Christian teaching would deal honorably and justly with their constituencies has been fulfilled.

. . . Both in America where Christians must lead the way for a wholesome internal policy and in the work of world reconstruction we must cultivate good intergroup relations. It must be done with precision tools not a blunt instrument. We have much in common with all who seek to exalt religion in a world that is threatened by materialism. As we inevitably move into areas of disagreement we should firmly state our case, for truth is partisan, but we must seek to establish the greatest possible degree of understanding and good will.

Another controversy touching church policy involves public education which is an indispensable force in maintaining our free way of life. Recent events require us to assert again our devotion to the principle of separation of church and state. These events also dramatize the failure of the public school system to lay strong foundations for Christian citizenship. A way must be found to use that system for fortifying Christian ideals as applied to civic life. Otherwise, we shall continue to be plagued by a situation that legalizes the teaching of an agnostic view of life and outlaws the teaching of a Christian view.

It presents a complex and delicate problem but not one that is beyond solution, and the alternatives to finding that solution are unthinkable. The public schools owe a debt to Christianity that can be discharged only by the placing of a positive emphasis upon the basic assumptions of Christianity, leaving to the denominations the interpretation of their distinctive tenets and cultivation of the individual's religious life. If we are afraid to attempt the laying out of a policy that imparts through public education the idea that attitudes and actions must be Christian if freedom survives, then the forces of secularism will continue to claim their advantage.

. . . We can replace war and exploitation with peace and human service if we move courageously into the political scene.

The business of politics is much more than manipulating mass sentiment for particular economic and social ends; it is one of the most satisfying expressions of faith in the efficacy of New Testament teachings.

Freedom of Religion

No study of the meaning of democracy would be adequate without an emphasis upon freedom of worship. The constitutional guarantee that this privilege shall not be invaded is so much a part of our lives that we seldom stop to think of the conditions which produced it. Too often we think in negative terms. Perhaps we gained an impression from textbooks that the framers of the Constitution merely concluded that, since the idea of a state-controlled church had not worked well in the old world or in the colonies, we would have none of that concept in the new Federal Government. To be sure, the policy of our nation is definite on the point that we will not have an official religion. Separation of church and state is one of our distinctive contributions to the science of government.

But the First Amendment to the Constitution says something else about the place of religious faith in American life. Here are its words: "Congress shall make no law respecting an establishment of religion, or prohibiting the free exercise thereof." In stressing the free exercise of faith, Thomas Jefferson, the author of this amendment, so richly endowed with spiritual insight, was thinking not in governmental terms but rather of the individual citizen, his right to spiritual growth and his privilege of religious expression, which should not be impaired.

In prohibiting a tax-supported church, the Constitution represents a break with the past; but it represents, also, the hopes and the dreams of the past for complete freedom for the human spirit.

It was a daring thing that our forefathers did, this assertion

NOTE: Address to National Association of Broadcasters, 1950. Published in *Liberty*, second quarter, 1951.

that the new government should not control the patterns of worship and religious belief. The wise men who designed the Constitution were determined that the tremendous power of organized religion should never be used to inhibit the individual in relation to his Creator.

The First Amendment to the Constitution is, therefore, one of the most significant instruments in history. There are two facets, and both must be viewed with understanding. First, the framers had a distrust of man; they recognized his frailty, and this applied not only to politicians and military men who had misused power; it applied even to the ministers. No man, according to this philosophy, could be trusted with power over the minds of his fellow man. But, again, the First Amendment represents something besides distrust of man. Its positive aspect explains the reverence we have for it. It reveals a high opinion of man as God's creation. It encourages individual faith.

In granting full freedom of worship, the authors revealed a faith that men would not abuse the privilege, that social stability would not be lost in the renunciation of control over religious forms. The Constitution reflects a faith that individual judgments in the supremely important issues of human life and destiny would not have a destructive impact. The authors dared to trust the individual in this vital realm of life.

Thus it should be clear that our democratic ideal of religious freedom is not in disparagement of religion. Our governmental foundations are essentially spiritual. George Washington spoke for the young nation when he said in his farewell address that decency and morality in public life are not possible without the inspiration of religion. The American policy, however, allows the citizen to seek an outlet for this divinely given right in ways that appeal to him, so that each man worships God according to the dictates of his own conscience.

We even allow each to reserve to himself the privilege of not worshiping at all if he chooses not to do so. The resources of a positive faith recognized by the Constitution will save the nation from any theoretical damage by those of infirm faith; they, too, must be protected.

It is an experiment, this American plan, but 161 years have proved its wisdom. We, the succeeding generations of Americans who have benefited by the cherished tradition, are sure that upon such a foundation of freedom and reverence for the individual the Republic will endure.

❖

The Prayer Room

Mr. Speaker: I have been asked by many Members to give the location of the Prayer Room and I would like to give directions as to how to reach it: Turn left at the rotunda on this level, and the first door on the left as you go west from the rotunda opens into the Prayer Room. It is open for inspection today and tomorrow by Members of the House and Senate only, but on Thursday, Friday, Saturday, and Sunday the Speaker has authorized me to say it may be seen by your friends and by the public. After that it will be used, of course, under the rules of the House by Members.

I know you are going to find it a very attractive room furnished and decorated in accordance with the finest traditions of our country.

. . . It would be impossible, Mr. Speaker, to mention all who have had a part in this enterprise, which has been completely nonpartisan from its conception.

NOTE: *Congressional Record*, House of Representatives, March 22, 1955.

. . . Representatives of the press have at all stages co-operated in undertaking to interpret adequately the establishment of this room.

Among many items of interest which historical research has produced is that in the early days when there were few meeting houses in Washington, religious services were occasionally conducted in the Capitol. It was a wise decision, however, to limit the use of the chapel to individual meditation and prayer. It will meet a deeply felt need. It is this practical service that should have emphasis, though I do not disparage its value as a symbol of our nation's faith. The manner in which it has been accomplished is of itself significant, for it has been in keeping with our greatest principles. It symbolizes our devotion to freedom of worship and the ideal of tolerance. The American doctrine, which has often been acclaimed in faraway places of the world, is not based upon indifference to religion. Our forefathers were men of great spiritual insight. While sectarianism sometimes found expression here, there was much that was held in common as the patterns of our Government were being fashioned. The founders of the Republic, for example, believed in God, in the dignity and worth of the individual, in the Golden Rule, in the spirit of brotherhood, and in justice and liberty as spiritual qualities in our common life. This faith is evident in our early documents: in the first words of the Mayflower Compact, "In the name of God, Amen"; and in the thrilling words of the Declaration of Independence which avow that all men are created equal and endowed by their Creator with inalienable rights. And just one month ago today we heard read in this Chamber the Farewell Address of George Washington containing these words:

"Of all the dispositions and habits which lead to political prosperity, religion and morality are indispensable supports.

In vain would that man claim the tribute of patriotism, who should labor to subvert these great pillars of human happiness, these firmest props of the duties of men and citizens. The mere politician, equally with the pious man, ought to respect and to cherish them."

It is fitting, Mr. Speaker, that the central figure in the chapel window is George Washington kneeling in prayer.

. . . Our differences are important, they are profound and fundamental, but in differing with our fellow Americans we respect each other. The one faith to which I have alluded sustains us in the present crisis. In our diversity there is unity, and it is found in our feeling that this nation has a glorious destiny to serve. There will doubtless be prayers of thanksgiving for this truth in the petitions offered in the little room. They should be offered with humility and reverence. No plans can be laid within its walls for the dissemination throughout the world of this devotion to universal love and good will. But surely in myriad ways other peoples can find evidence that we have no purposes in the world to serve which conflict with their greatest and highest good.

. . . The story of the Prayer Room will be printed, and the official chapter of its establishment will be closed, but we trust that its contribution to our well-being and that of our beloved country will be a continuing one.

. . . The room is done in tones of blue. The rug is dark blue; the simple armchairs are upholstered in a lighter blue leather; the walls are of a pastel shade.

On the altar made of white oak is an open Bible and, at the base of the window, two vases of freshly cut flowers from the Botanic Garden.

The chapel is illuminated by shielded wall lights and two seven-pronged candelabra which are placed before the altar, one on each side.

Directly in front of each candelabrum is a prie-dieu, also made of white oak.

The American flag stands in one corner as a symbol of our freedom of worship.

The central feature of the room, the stained glass window, was donated anonymously by a group of designers and craftsmen from a studio in California's 21st Congressional District. Their thought in designing and fabricating the window was "to give it as a thank offering to this country and to dedicate it to those men who have in the past sought God's guidance and to those who presently determine the destiny of this nation by the inspiration of their decisions."

In the center medallion, on a background of carefully selected ruby glass from England, France, and Germany, is the kneeling figure of George Washington, representing the people of the United States in fervent prayer. Etched behind the figure are the words of the first verse of Psalm 16: "Preserve me, O God: for in thee do I put my trust." The main body of the window is composed of glass made in West Virginia and Indiana.

The upper medallion represents the reverse side of the Great Seal of the United States on which appear the phrases *annuit coeptis* (he [God] has favored our undertakings) and *novus ordo seclorum* (a new order of the ages); the obverse side of the Seal is represented in the lower medallion. Immediately below the upper medallion is the inscription, "This Nation under God."

In the background are shown thirteen stars and the names of the original states. The border has been formed of a laurel wreath with the names of the other states of the Union. Space has been left for one more state. Others can be added by cutting across the laurel border and inserting a nameplate.

In the two corners are shown a book and a candle, representing the Holy Scriptures and the quotation of verse 105 of Psalm 119: "Thy word is a lamp unto my feet, and a light unto my path."

❖

Building a Christian World

This is more of a testimony than a speech. One of my friends said, "Brooks, it's too bad the Baptists abandoned testimony meetings. You love to talk so much that if we could have preserved those meetings you would have had an outlet and wouldn't have had to go into politics to find a forum. We could have saved you for an honorable career." I want to speak briefly about the place that my church has had in my work as a professional worker in the field of government. Not that I expect my function as chairman of the Christian Life Commission to become involved at all in the political demands that are upon me as a representative in the Congress, but because I believe in maintaining the bridge between these two great communities—our Christian community and the political community.

The state must never be held in contempt merely because frail men perform imperfectly as political craftsmen, and the fallacy must be banished that the church has nothing to do with political action. There have been some fateful decisions in the past, and our Baptists have been in the forefront of many a struggle for precious spiritual values in the life of the state. The ideal of freedom, for example, is basic, and whenever those struggles for freedom were fresh in the minds

NOTE: Speech as chairman of the Christian Life Commission to the Southern Baptist Convention, Kansas City, Missouri, May 31, 1956.

of Baptists, they knew that they would neglect government
—its stability and righteousness—at their peril. Our forefathers
had a very good phrase for it: "the free church in the free
state." And so, if we were concerned about only our institutional survival, we would view the state as a workshop and we
would be concerned about the kind of political institutions
under which we live.

. . . The Christian Life Commission would never undertake to speak for millions of Baptists. Now and then with a
special mandate such as the attack upon alcoholism, we
have spoken to legislative bodies in a representative capacity.
But we realize that the effectiveness of our work in the final
analysis will be measured in the quality of the congregation's life. We propose to be a channel of information and of
inspiration to those who struggle to build Christian communities, to make the life of the community safer and more enriching for young people who are baffled by many new problems.

We act with recognition of the fact that the method as well
as the goal is important and that democratic standards must
be adhered to. We believe that since ours is a broad fellowship
and embraces so many points of view, we should not press for
political action unless a clear mandate has been given us.
Nevertheless, we believe that it would be a betrayal of our
faith ever to dilute our moral influence for the sake of expediency. We abhor moral mediocrity. Christian ministers who
must maintain constant scrutiny over the political life of the
nation should always be brave enough, whatever the embarrassment in terms of economic pressure, to speak boldly where
moral issues are involved. I would rather my church would
be wrong than to say it has no message for a world that needs
every urge to righteousness.

Baptists have made some great decisions in the past when

moral values were at stake. There was a time when authoritarianism threatened us, but we met it intelligently. There was the situation in which—and I suppose that this is essentially theological—there was a time when we had to get rid of the narrow restrictions that a questionable concept of predestinarianism placed upon us. Our campaigns for evangelism and world missions would have been inhibited had we not broken with the past. So, in milestone decisions the Baptists have stood for a progressive and dynamic position. And today, when we are having to make vital decisions in the political and governmental community, we need that same clear prophetic voice and that same boldness of purpose. And I can tell you tonight, as I come from Washington to have this fine comradeship with you, that I am heartened by the things that I see and hear in this Convention hall, by the knowledge that our people are united essentially in our devotion to the things that really matter.

. . . We must take up the cause of world peace. It is significant that in attendance at the Convention are some of our fellow Baptists from Russia. My responsibilities as a member of the House Foreign Affairs Committee sometimes give me a grim picture of our relations with Communist governments. Ours is a divided world. If it becomes a united world, it will be through the contribution of men and women of good will. Someday if we are continually effective, all governments will build their structure upon the concepts of good will and Christian love.

. . . Some of the most important things that took place in the United Nations General Assembly, in which I was privileged to participate, were in the lobbies and in the delegates' lounge where we gathered as individuals and often as fellow Christians, to talk about a lasting peace.

. . . In all of our literature the idea of a new birth and the commitment of an individual are receiving prominence, and closely related is the idea of individual responsibility for contributing to the building of a Christian world. Every man may thus help answer his own prayer that God's will may be done on earth as it is in heaven. God has committed the governing of this planet to us, and has prescribed that all governmental powers are a sacred trust. Christ's words to Pilate, "You would have no power at all except it were given you from above," are addressed to all in authority. It becomes our Christian duty to seek an ordering of this world's life that will make more likely a favorable decision in the soul struggle that every man experiences. And each man finds that the contribution he makes to the world supplies moral exercise that he requires.

I should like to allude to something that is of great importance—the establishment of racial harmony. Our colored brethren, motivated by the same loyalties that direct us, recognize that we of the churches are trying to provide moral leadership; and while the problem is very difficult and very delicate, we as Christians can at least attempt in our congregations and in our communities to create an atmosphere in which the right solutions may be sought. For it is my judgment that doctrinaire attitudes will not solve it; only Christian attitudes can help us now.

One of my friends said to me the other day, "I hope you will not be a victim of the idea that only the white people are excited and lacking calmness in this hour. Our colored people are concerned, too." He added, "They are marching through a tunnel; they see light ahead. Never place any rocks in the way, and if rocks are shutting off the light, remove the rocks so that they see light ahead." That is good counsel. And we of the Christian faith must do our best to keep that light ahead so that they may march through the tunnel out of the darkness into a bright and promising day. I replied, "We, too, we of the majority group are in a tunnel. God's children everywhere, beset by the problems of disease and poverty and evil, are in a tunnel, and it is the light of Christian hope that the Bible and the Christian message gives us."

These are some of the severe problems that we wrestle with in the Christian Life Commission, but we are not disconsolate. We know that the resources of our mighty denomination are here at hand. We know they are available, and above everything, we know that the promises of God himself are clear. I have no doubt about the outcome, knowing that I have done my best with my fellow workers in this important commission. I have no doubt about the outcome because I read in God's Word this simple promise: "Fear not, little flock; it is the Father's good pleasure to give you the kingdom."

❖

Meet Your President

Mr. Chairman, first I want to express my profound gratitude for the great honor my fellow Baptists have given me. I have been elected to Congress eight times, but none of those elections brought either the excitement or the surprise produced by the Chicago Convention action.

The committee lists this part of the program: "Meet your president." You are doubtless wondering just what kind of fellow the messengers voted into office. You are entitled to know a little more about me. Even the youngest among you

Note: First speech as president of Southern Baptist Convention to its Executive Committee, Nashville, Tennessee, June 19, 1957.

have probably attended more conventions than I have. I am awfully new at this kind of job and I need your help. Most of you are ministers, and I particularly appeal to you.

I was asked once by a preacher friend, "What is your work in Congress like?" I told him that it resembles the minister's; it has pastoral and prophetic aspects. A mother wants to know about her son in the army, or Dad wants him discharged to help make a crop. Some menial service, some footwork, going down to the departments, is a routine matter. I am a pastor looking after my flock. Then sometimes I assume the role of the prophet. Whether I fill that role well is a question, but I attempt it now and then. Whether pastor or prophet, whether in the role of servant or instructor, your work resembles mine.

I judge from the invitations I get that you intend to make me pay for this honor. It reminds me of the Ozark mountaineer who told his friend in Russellville about their church troubles. I hasten to add that it was before the moral tone of the church in that area became as high as today. "That good for nothing trifling preacher of ours run off with $200 of the church's money." "Did you catch him?" "Yep, we got him. He was on his way to Little Rock but we brought him back." "Did you get your money back?" "Nope, but we're making him preach it out—ever last penny of it!"

. . . I must tell you something about myself that I trust will not shock you. You may have a controversial president on your hands. Knowing how you feel about controversy in a group as large as ours with its diversity of views and interests, of political philosophies and economic and social attitudes, I can understand how this might be a rather frightening reference. I hope I shall not embarrass you. I assure you I shall not invite controversy, but I am determined to be my natural self and I may be drawn into controversy merely by doing what I regard as my duty to you. But please look at it this way. It would be better for me to be controversial because of a conviction than to avoid controversy in a way that would give you *cause* to be ashamed of me.

. . . I propose to be a *democratic* president. If Baptists are distinguished historically by devotion to anything, I believe it is the ideal of democracy, though today we share it with many other religious communities. Our democratic practices grow out of our concept of the competence of the individual. We should repudiate all forms of authoritarianism, even incipient types that occasionally threaten Baptist bodies. Let us be alert to protect our tradition. Embraced in this idea is the cherished right of dissent, and let us respect it not only because of our reverence for the individual but also for the reason that the cause of truth is served by the nonconformist applying critical judgments to sharpen and improve our denominational standards. Organizations which grow as rapidly as ours constantly have to re-examine their procedures to determine if this ideal is being maintained. The Convention is now so large that we would do well to alter our procedures to make sure there will be grass roots participation in policy decisions.

. . . We should not be satisfied until there is a clear and affirmative answer to the question, "Do Baptists reflect the compassion of God for the multitudes?"

One of the thrilling references to Jesus is that "the common people heard him gladly." Where his words are well conveyed in this century, he will be heard gladly by young people and old people, black people and white people, poor people and well-off people, working people and professional people, rural people and city people, for his words were uttered for all.

Our foreign mission program is grounded in this idea of the Christian's responsibility for the masses of other continents as well as our own. When Jesus directed his disciples to be witnesses not only in Jerusalem and Judea and Samaria but in the uttermost part of the earth, he sent them out not to explore territory or assert sovereignty or conserve physical values, but "to preach the gospel to the poor, . . . to heal the brokenhearted, to preach deliverance to the captives." Where people live his followers should go.

. . . Secondly, our Baptist program must be three-dimensional. Qualitative as well as quantitative measurements of progress must be used. We have made no small plans. The Jubilee goal of 30,000 new churches and mission stations will challenge us. I believe, however, that there is sufficient vigor and imagination to attain this and our new membership goals as well. At the same time, we must attend to the requirements of the resolution sponsored by Dr. Paul Caudill and unanimously approved by the 1957 Convention. The program must have not only length and breadth, but depth. Bible reading, strengthened prayer life, and daily Christian living must be urged upon our millions of constituents. Greatness cannot spring out of impressive statistics or institutional efficiency. The moral power that comes with individual sacrifice must be fully felt in Baptist ranks.

❖

My Trip to Russia

We reached the Baptist Church in Moscow at 8:45 A.M. to find a long line of people waiting outside, and a number of American news services represented. The church was filled

NOTE: Brief report on visit to Moscow Baptist Church, Sunday, April 20, 1958.

to capacity already and as our group moved down the aisle, the crowd flowed in behind us and filled every available space. The church auditorium was smaller than I had anticipated, but I believe some 2,000 of the 4,000-member congregation were present that day.

It was the most amazing sight I have ever witnessed in a church. Although the pastors say that 20 per cent of the congregation is made up of young people, and I did see some young people in front, the large majority of the congregation were women and elderly men. Most of them appeared to be from the poor classes, but among them were some fairly well dressed men and women. A very attractively dressed choir led magnificent singing. A number was announced at once, and it seemed that every person in the congregation was singing. Several wiped their eyes. The special anthems were unusually good. Apparently considerable emphasis is given to music.

Behind a high pulpit in large letters were the Russian words for "God is love." There was an eagerness in the faces of the congregation (pathos in some) that was deeply moving. When Brother Karev introduced me, I sensed that the crowd gasped at the mention of our eight and a half million Southern Baptists.

First, I presented the two Bibles and six Testaments in the Russian language as a symbol of our love and good will. I told them that I am not an ordained minister so would not preach a sermon but would only give a testimony. My intourist interpreter stumbled on the word "testimony" and asked if "little talk" would be satisfactory.

I spoke of my early church life and then I commented that I had come thousands of miles, the farthest I had ever been from home, to be with them. I assured them that I would go back a better man by reason of this experience, and

I meant it! Their faces—their songs—their humility—their friendliness—their warmth—all combined to impress me with the significance of their faith under these circumstances. They have suffered, yet they have faith in the gospel. The ease with which they went through the service, participating enthusiastically in it, some even standing for several hours, set a good example for Baptists in our country.

I turned to ask if they sang "Amazing Grace." Karev did not know it and he asked me to sing a little of it, which I did. He then said they did not know it. I was disappointed because I wanted to hear a hymn I was familiar with, but before the service ended we all joined in singing, "God be with you till we meet again."

Then they waved handkerchiefs at us, and when the benediction was said the people moved out of the aisles to the outside so that we could make our exit. But nearly everyone wanted to shake hands.

Having witnessed this demonstration of great devotion, I won't complain ever again if I have to stand to hear a service. I want to dedicate myself more completely than ever to the simple things we stand for. My Christian witness took on a new meaning that day.

❖

This World: A Christian's Workshop

Before sketching briefly some of my activities as your president and submitting some recommendations for you to consider, let me say a word of appreciation for the great honor

NOTE: President's Address to the Southern Baptist Convention, Houston, Texas, May 20, 1958.

you conferred upon me a year ago. To be president of this Convention is both an exciting adventure and an exalted privilege. I thank you from the bottom of my heart for this enriching experience and for the opportunity of Christian service which you have afforded me. I began attending Baptist conventions fifty years ago. In 1908 my mother took me to Fort Smith to the Arkansas state convention and it made a lasting impression upon my boyish mind. I saw that great and stalwart Texas Baptist, Dr. J. B. Gambrell, on the platform and heard his pungent comments on Baptist service. Of course I never dreamed that one day my name would be listed a few lines below his among the Convention presidents. The first Southern Baptist Convention I ever attended was presided over by Dr. Gambrell in the city of Washington in 1920. As a Treasury Department clerk, attending law classes at night, I slipped away to one of the Convention meetings as an observer and was thrilled by what I saw and heard.

You have been tolerant of my deficiencies during these twelve months. I have been constantly aware of two things about my background that did not fit the usual pattern for the Convention presidency. I am a layman. Second, I am in the service of a government which is institutionally independent of all religious societies. In retrospect, I can say something with which I believe you will concur: To be a layman is not of itself a handicap. The rank and file of Baptist men in the South are conscious of the fact that the choice of a layman represented a drawing together of ministers and men—of the ordained and the unordained—and for this I am grateful. On occasions I have needed professional help, and always I have found it available in spontaneous and generous measure. I know that Baptist laymen would want me to say in their behalf that there is deep affection and admiration in their hearts for our dedicated ministers.

The biggest event in our year, according to Baptist editors, was the launching of our Jubilee program under the direction of my beloved predecessor, Dr. C. C. Warren. I have tried to give full support to this great undertaking and to provide an accurate interpretation of it in my talks across the country. At one point I was able to devote a few minutes to the subject on a coast-to-coast TV program that would have cost us in excess of $30,000 had we been purchasing the time. I have not been timid in seizing publicity opportunities for our Baptist cause.

During the past twelve months I have journeyed in the Convention's interest from Hamilton, Ontario, to Houston, and from Los Angeles to Moscow. I was able to attend five state conventions and innumerable local and district meetings. First in importance in the many tasks I have had was to participate in efforts to preserve our unity in a period of tension, to hold together our scattered congregations in this hour of the world's supreme need. A common faith continues to bind us together. Territorial expansion has, of course, produced interesting new diversities. The problems of California, for example, are quite different from those of our Georgia brethren. Social conditions surrounding Baptist workers in Louisiana vary greatly from those discovered by our representatives in the exciting new outpost in New York City. It is a great tribute to the skill of those who have fashioned this voluntary assembly called the Southern Baptist Convention and a confirmation of the soundness of the basic principles which underlie Baptist polity. Only in great flexibility can Christian fellowship be found in this complex twentieth century. . . . In a year of controversy I have been able to look up with deep gratitude to my brethren, both those who differ and those who agree with me, for having spoken the truth in love.

. . . I find in the minutes of the 1915 Houston Convention a message from Negro Baptists simultaneously holding their convention at Danville, Virginia. This message, coupled with a long and deeply moving report of our own 1915 Convention's committee on work among Negroes, served to remind me that this task of helping the minority racial group is also a continuing one. Some of the tragic governmental conflicts involving race have obscured the fact that there are proven and accepted ways by which Southern Baptists may express their Christian concern for the minority's welfare and progress.

During my unforgettable evening with the Mississippi Baptists in their state convention, I heard reports of the work being done in that state in behalf of ministerial training for the Negroes. It was a splendid demonstration of what can be accomplished in that field. I am not suggesting, of course, that traditional methods will always suffice. It would be well for us to recognize that imagination must accompany our compassion.

. . . It is not my purpose in this report to dwell upon the complexities of the problem of race or other social issues. I realize that we cannot have complete unanimity in these matters, but it would be tragic for us to assume that we can function as a Christian body without assigning to trusted representatives of the Convention the task of pointing out our Christian duty with respect to social evils and current conflicts. The Christian Life Commission has a dual role to fill. It is authorized to speak for Southern Baptists where specific mandates are given, as in the case of legislation affecting advertising of alcoholic beverages and the suppression of obscene literature upon the newsstands of America. Equally important is its role of familiarizing our people with problems of this nature, supplying counsel and advice on the subject as well as information on the scriptural teaching in specific areas, and to seek a sensitizing of the Christian conscience wherever evil, injustice, and oppression exist anywhere in the world. The problems of environment must be considered—if for no other reason, because our institutional survival requires it. . . .

We shall continue to struggle for an incorruptible state and a Christian society—not to relieve ourselves of the obligations of Christian education, which equips the individual to meet the recurring temptations of life. We know that finally it will be, not the absence of allurements in the world that redeems men, but the integrity that springs from transforming spiritual experiences. We owe it to our youth to improve their environment, but any young man is best fortified when, nurtured by a powerful religious influence, he is able to purpose in his heart, as Daniel did, not to defile himself. We seek not to dominate but to influence the state, and we will send our sons and daughters into the world with a sense of Christian vocation. The Christian and the patriot may dwell in the same heart, but only if the patriot acknowledges the universality of faith and love and repels the chauvinist. The generosity with which we support our home and foreign mission programs testifies to our willingness to accept world responsibilities.

. . . One of the most inspiring experiences of the year was my visit to the grave of our beloved Dr. George W. Truett. It was in the mood of rededication that I stood in silence, recalling some of the eloquent words I had heard him use. I learned first from him literature's most devotional lines outside the Bible, the moving words of St. Augustine, "Thou hast made me for thyself, and my soul will not rest until it rests, O God, in thee." I remembered how he warned against the pressures of materialism with a simple incident, the anonymous note handed to him: "Pray for a young man who is getting rich very fast." Prosperity is, comparatively, a new experience for Baptists. As we pray for a denomination that is getting rich very fast, may we determine to use our power with nobility and wisdom.

I recalled, too, the new resolutions that I had made as I heard him speak of our mission on this earth. God did not propose to detract, Dr. Truett said, from the critical importance of this earthly existence. In boyhood, I had avoided confusion on this subject by assuming that when a minister said that I should despise the world he meant I should despise worldliness. The Bible told me that God loved the world, and I thrilled to the song "This Is My Father's World." So in Dr. Truett's words were confirmation of the idea that *this world is a Christian's workshop.*